LMS STEAM
AT EUSTON & CAMDEN

LOCO-SPOTTING
IN THE 1950s & 1960s

ROD STEELE

AMBERLEY

THE
ROYAL SCOT
WEEKDAYS

NORTHBOUND

LONDON (EUSTON)   dep 10 0 am
GLASGOW (CENTRAL) arr 6 25 pm

SOUTHBOUND

GLASGOW (CENTRAL) dep 10 0 am
LONDON (EUSTON)   arr 6 13 pm

BRITISH RAILWAYS

First published 2013

Amberley Publishing
The Hill, Stroud
Gloucestershire, GL5 4EP

www.amberley-books.com

British Library Cataloguing in Publication Data.
A catalogue record for this book is available from the British Library.

ISBN 978 1 4456 3268 1
eBook ISBN 9781 4456 3279 7

Typeset in 10pt on 13pt Sabon.
Typesetting and Origination by Amberley Publishing.
Printed in the UK.

Contents

Introduction
Underlining LMS Steam

During school holidays and at weekends in the 1950s and early 1960s, youngsters – and some adults – gathered on station platforms all over the country. The object of their attention was steam locomotives, every sighting carefully logged in either a notebook or the must-have Ian Allan *ABC* loco-spotters' books, the traditional method of recording a sighting to underline the number and name of each locomotive – hence the title of this introduction. For the price of a platform ticket, or at open platforms for no cost, you could experience the sight and smell of steam engines.

At London Euston, a terminus, you were permitted a close-up vantage of the region's titled premier express trains both departing and arriving, most of which were headed by a named engine. The majority of photographs in *LMS Steam at Euston & Camden* are of the majestic Duchesses, the powerful rebuilt Royal Scots, and the numerous Jubilees – engines designed under the auspices of the LMS Chief Engineer Sir William A. Stanier F.R.S.

Although London Midland Region steam engines could easily be seen at Euston, access to Camden Shed proved near impossible, the shed master's office immediately beyond the pedestrian entrance. Trespassers risked prosecution. The only way around this necessitated applying for a special permit weeks in advance.

Parents regarded the loco-spotting of their offspring as a harmless, safe hobby getting them out of the house. Heritage railways recreate that lost scene on a much smaller scale over half a century later. I hope the 190 or so photos here will evoke happy memories for readers. *RS*

Opposite: The sleek lines of the *Duchess of Hamilton* of the LMS Coronation class.

When Euston station opened in 1837, the departure and arrivals platforms were each served by two lines of track. Note the absence of locomotives as a cable system was used to haul trains up the Camden Incline until 1844.

London Euston

Today's travellers through London's Euston station will have no concept of what it looked like in what are referred to as the 'steam days'. Opened by the London & Birmingham Railway Company on 20 July 1837, it was the first mainline station in the capital. Given inaugural status, the project suffered from not having a model to base a station upon.

The company announced its presence to the world by having architect Phillip Hardwick create a Doric arch which would forever be known as the Euston Arch, no doubt an attempt to suggest that this is 'the gateway to the North'. An elaborate Great Hall, over 125 feet long and 62 feet wide, opened in 1849, its ornate ceiling rising to 64 feet. Two staircases led up to the shareholders' meeting room, with the figure of Britannia gazing down from above the door. A marble statue of George Stephenson stood at the foot of the stairs.

In spite of enormous expense on impressive architecture, locos did not reach the station's two platforms for the first seven years on account of the steepness of Camden Bank. The trains were attached to cables from stationary winding engine and brakemen controlled the descent of arrivals.

Euston soon expanded; more land was purchased to increase the number of platforms to fifteen (with a turntable hidden behind a wall on Platform 15). Human remains had to be removed from the burial ground of the St James church on the Cardington Street side of the station to create a departures site.

Raising the canopy over the arrivals platforms by a further six feet improved ventilation, and this was achieved by using jacks and inserting new ironwork at the column bases. The departure platform surfaces did not reflect the station's grandeur, however. They were made of wooden planking and this remained in place on several platforms until the late 1950s. Passenger facilities encompassed two new hotels – Euston Hotel West and East Wings – constructed on Drummond Street. W. H. Smith opened its first bookstall at Euston in 1848, paving the way for outlets at other stations.

The outbreak of both the First and Second World Wars postponed any plans for major alterations at Euston. Then in 1963 the station was demolished in favour of a dull concrete structure typical of 1960s modernist architecture. The result was a much criticised change of character. Unfortunately the transition neglected to preserve any of the original station structures although the siting of the Great Hall and Arch proved a handicap that could not be overcome. Both were demolished. Two smaller

Postcard of LNWR locomotive at Euston
c. 1905.

Left: British Railways poster featuring the
Mid-Day Scot.

Opposite: Designed by Philip Hardwick,
Euston's famous arch stood 72 feet high.
It was demolished in the 1960s as part of the
station's total rebuild

buildings dating from 1874 can be seen on the Euston Road. These Portland stone lodges feature engravings of destinations accessible via the station (albeit destinations sometimes necessitating several changes of trains) and fortunately they still exist in superb condition.

Euston's status as the major station on the Midland Region originated with the London & Birmingham Railway Company, which was incorporated into the London & North Western Railway Company in 1846. A subsequent re-grouping of the railway companies in 1923 created the 'Big Four' (the Great Western Railway, the Southern Railway, the London & North Eastern Railway, and the London Midland & Scottish Railway). All four of these companies evolved into British Railways upon the post-war nationalisation in 1948.

Much to the delight of spotters, locos of the Duchess, Princess, Royal Scot, and Jubilee classes all carried names and Euston remained 'the place' in London to observe motive power on the region's premier express trains. Patriot class engines in original and rebuilt form, most of them named, and Black Fives also made an appearance.

Spotters usually congregated on Platforms 1 and 2. Platform tickets were not required. You could simply walk in off the street to gain access to Platforms 1 to 4, each designated for arrivals of express trains such as The Royal Scot, The Irish Mail, and The Mancunian. At the country end of these platforms, the Ampthill Square road bridge backdrop graced a splendid panorama as majestic Duchesses, Royal Scots, Jubilees, and Princesses completed their journeys.

Parcels vehicles of differing vintage occupied the country end of Platform 1, a clutter of incoming parcels noticeable on trolleys as the Inwards Parcels Office and Railway

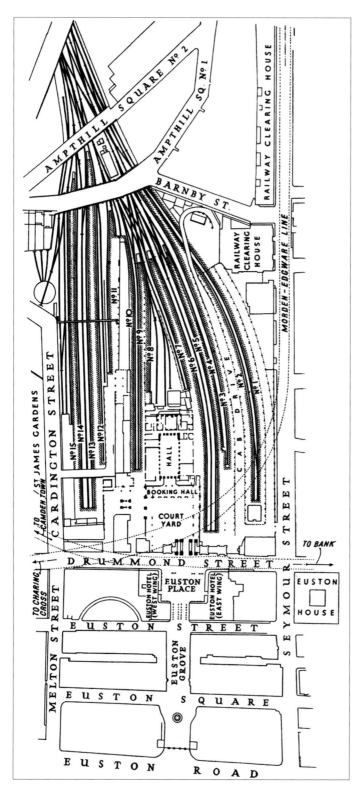

Plan of Euston in 1938,
published to mark the
station's centenary.
North is at the top of
the page.

Opposite: Jubilee
No. 45555 *Quebec*.

Clearing House were situated here. A Scammell Scarab tractor unit with chequered sides denoted its use as the inter-station parcels service. And black cabs – a mixture of the familiar post-war Austin three-door open luggage FX3 type and the subsequent four-door FX4 design which was an integral factor of the 1950s London transport scene – streamed to and from a taxi rank in between Platforms 2 and 3.

Advertisements in the form of colourful wall-mounted enamel signs for products the like of Stephen's Inks and Palethorpe's sausages, or posters for Pepsident toothpaste, Osram light-bulbs and Camp Coffee, crowded around the buffer barrier enclosures on Platforms 1 and 2. At intervals, the much sought after site of the clock above Platform 1 advertised the Phoenix Assurance, Fenner V belts and Ecko Vision – a firm supplying televisions. A big red sign above Platform 2 highlighted the location of the Great Hall, the cafeterias and buffets. (Was it just my imagination or did the British Rail signs at Euston appear a brighter red than those at other stations?)

Parcel trains and suburban Watford electric commuter services ran into the centre of the station. Platform 6 saw use in the instance of occasional royal visits, the station master's office being an ideal position to oversee the events, the station master in his top hat and tails.

Some spotters also experienced the hustle and bustle of departures for the minor expense of a platform ticket, which was valid for about an hour (though seldom checked on exiting). A cherry red sign stated 'Platforms 12 to 15. Passengers This Way'. Under this another sign proudly announced 'The Royal Scot Departs Daily from Platform 13'.

Countless photographs depict the ends of Platforms 1 and 2, showing Stanier locos simmering at buffer stops. This photo by the author of Platforms 1 and 2, taken in November 2012, might easily be mistaken for an underground car park.

The way enthusiasts prefer to remember Euston, in all its glory in the 1950s. By 1963, steam had made way for diesel. Electric train haulage followed in 1966. *(Gresley Society)*

Euston station today:
Above, the 1960s airport-style frontage and station entrance.

Right: One of the surviving pair of gate lodges at Euston. The inscriptions list the main towns and cities served by the LNWR.
(John Christopher)

The Night Mail

A book on Euston would not be complete without mention of the famous night mail service, the Down West Coast Postal Special to give the service its full title, although railway men referred to it simply as 'the Postal'.

Every evening at 7.00 p.m. a 1A Willesden engine brought the night mail stock into arrivals Platform 2. Casual observers might not have noticed that this fourteen coach formation was not for passengers. Five of the coaches were equipped for sorting and had catchers to collect mail from line-side equipment, sorted mail swinging out to be snatched by pick-up nets along the West Coast Main Line. The other nine coaches stored the mail sacks.

Lights on the left side of the carriages enabled crew to make out the pick-up points en route. Instead of a British Rail logo, the red coaching stock displayed 'Royal Mail' in letters twelve inches high, with a royal monogram between the two words. A post-box slot in a carriage side also distinguished postal trains from any others. This service incurred a surcharge of half a penny, or ½d in pre-decimal money.

General Post Office (GPO) vans delivered sacks of mail, some already sorted, from the London area to be loaded onto the night mail train. They parked on the taxi road along Platform 2. Around fifty GPO employees on the train itself sorted the mail into location-labelled pigeon holes, each sorter having an allocation of forty-eight pigeon holes. Once readied, mail sacks were wrapped in strong, tightly bound leather pouches fit for the purpose of offloading at speed.

A 5A Crewe North-based Pacific always headed the night mail train to Crewe, departing at 8.30 p.m. for the first section of the journey. Five stops took place en-route for manual loading and unloading, the first at Rugby eighty-two miles from Euston for four minutes, then Tamworth for nine minutes, followed by Crewe for sixteen minutes, Preston for ten and, finally, Carlisle for ten minutes.

An initial change of engine took place at Crewe while postal workers loaded further mail on board. The second engine change occurred at Carlisle preceding the crossing of the border into Scotland. Punctuality, rather than speed, was paramount given the requirement to connect with mail trains from other regions.

Small huts at the end of narrow paths housed postmen awaiting 'the Postal' at each of the thirty-three exchange points marking its route, sets of steps outside for the purpose of both loading outgoing and collecting incoming mail. At the apt moment, the men, standing well clear of the track in anticipation of the train's distinctive string of side lights, extended the arms of the line side catchers. Meanwhile, a look-out on the train kept watch for the chequered board signaling exactly when to extend the hook and net. The mechanical arms firstly picked up incoming mail which detached into a net extended from the train. A second arm, this with outgoing mail was also extended. It connected with another line side catcher that detached the pouch into a trackside net. Several thuds could be heard as the equipment connected and the sacks of mail were propelled into the waiting line-side net, while the other catcher delivered incoming mail into the nets on board the train.

After the stop at Carlisle, coaches were detached to link up with other trains, with more coaches then attached for Scotland. Arrival in Glasgow Central was at 5.27 a.m. The final exchange of mail was in October 1971, and the last Travelling Post Office special ran in January 2004. Afterwards the postal service changed over to road and air transport.

The black and white film *Night Mail*, sponsored by the GPO and made by the Crown Film Unit in 1936, faithfully recorded the pre-war LMS working of the train from Crewe northwards. Many people will be familiar with the W. H. Auden poem on the soundtrack that is rhythmically spoken to the beat of the engine.

> This is the night mail crossing the border,
> Bringing the cheque and the postal order,
> Letters for the rich, letters for the poor,
> The shop at the corner, the girl next door …

On 8 August 1963 the Down Postal special, by now diesel-hauled by D326, became headline news in newspapers and on the television. This train was brought to a halt by dummy signals installed by thieves at a quiet countryside location near Cheddington in Buckinghamshire. Now known as 'The Great Train Robbery', an estimated haul of £2.6 million in used banknotes was off-loaded from the train in a carefully planned operation.

The Spotters' Essential Reference Book

First published in 1942 and priced at one shilling and three pence, the four regional Ian Allan *ABC* books were updated twice yearly. By 1945 these volumes were clocking up sales of over 200,000 copies. The price increased to two shillings and six pence by the late 1950s, which was quite a sum at that time. These little books proved an essential purchase for spotters and were a bestseller during the post-war steam era, and the supplementary 'combined' all regions annual hardback edition became a prized item.

Now highly treasured by collectors, the high prices of unmarked copies offered for sale nowadays reflect their rarity as locos observed would have a line drawn under the names and numbers.

The *ABC* of British Railways Locomotives regional summer 1959 edition carried by loco spotters on the London Midland and Scottish region.

It listed loco Nos. 40000 – 59999 and 70000-99999. As 92250, a 9F 2-10-0, was the last numbered engine of the British Railways fleet, perhaps someone was optimistic about a future building programme.

The other three regions also had their own versions.

After this edition, gaps started to appear in listings as locomotives were being withdrawn. Within a few years the number of steam locomotives in use no longer warranted separate publications. Combined but much depleted versions with soft cover versions would later become the norm.

The 1955 spring and summer editions of regional *abc* books featured superb line drawings by A. N. Wolstenholme on their covers. In the late 1950s a photograph replaced the drawn covers.

Inside the book, twenty-four pages of small photographs gave a total of seventy-two illustrated locomotives. Latterly, paintings by Vic Welch graced the centre pages for several years until they too were superseded by colour photographs.

As with all the regional books the colour of the region was shown on the cover, and for the Midland Region red was chosen.

The last numbered engine in the books is 92096, followed by a note stating, 'Engines of this class are still being delivered'.

The Clan 4-6-0 class list numbers up to 72024, with proposed names proving very short-lived as the building programme came under review, and the series finished with 72009.

ABC book covers courtesy of Ian Allan Publishing.

Titled Train Departures
from Euston

SCOTLAND
The Royal Scot – to Glasgow Central
The Mid-Day Scot – to Glasgow Central
The Caledonian – to Glasgow Central
The Royal Highlander – (sleeping car train) to Perth, Aberdeen/Inverness

WALES
The Welshman – to Llandudno/ Pwllheli

IRELAND
The Irish Mail – via Holyhead
The Shamrock – via Liverpool Lime Street
The Emerald Isle Express – via Holyhead
The Ulster Express – via Fleetwood, later Heysham
The Northern Irishman – (sleeping car train) via Stranraer

WOLVERHAMPTON (HIGH LEVEL)
The Midlander

LIVERPOOL
The Merseyside Express – to Liverpool Lime Street
The Red Rose – to Liverpool Lime Street

Also Boat Train Specials:
Empress Voyager (when required)
Cunard Express (when required)
The Manxman (summers only)

MANCHESTER
The Mancunian – to Manchester London Road
The Comet – (via Stoke on Trent) to Manchester London Road
The Lancastrian – to Manchester London Road

THE LAKE DISTRICT
The Lakes Express – to Windermere

Pride of place in the named trains list are the most important – the Anglo-Scottish 10.00 a.m. and 1.00 p.m. departures of The Royal Scot and The Mid-Day Scot.

Although many trains had titles it was only in 1950 that British Railways introduced train headboards. The boards, made of aluminium (with one early exception), were designed to fit above the locomotive's smokebox door.

The London Midland's prestigious Royal Scot received the first headboard, and the original was made from wood and painted red with yellow lettering. The rectangular board had curved ends and a shield above with a Scottish lion rampant. Later versions of the same shape became more elaborate with tartan backgrounds which looked a work of art by the painter.

The only other of the region's titled trains to have a similar rectangular shaped headboard was The Caledonian when introduced in June 1957. The Caledonian had two shields: one with the cross of St George, the other the cross of St Andrew.

All other titled trains received the curved variety. Some with long names such as The Merseyside Express needed larger sized boards and three rows of letters instead of the normal two.

Standard colours for the backgrounds varied between red or black for English versions, Scottish versions painted blue, and The Northern Irishman predictably green.

The Royal Scot later had examples of the curved board in use together with original versions.

The only one not to have a curved version was The Caledonian, although several different versions on the same style appeared.

In addition to the headboards, coach destination boards with the name of the train and station of origin and destination were introduced. Three named trains also displayed ornate versions of the name on end coach tailboards: The Royal Scot, The Caledonian and The Red Rose.

The Shamrock to Liverpool Lime Street

The Mancunian to Manchester London Road

TYPICAL MID-1950s EUSTON TIMETABLE

Departures				Arrivals			

Departures				Arrivals			
0.02	Crewe	5A	RS				
0.020	Glasgow	1B	D				
0.030	Liverpool	8A	PR				
0.040	Manchester	8A	J				
				1.10	Crewe	5A	RS
1.37	Wolverhampton	9A	J	1.37	Birmingham	1B	J
				2.40	Liverpool	8A	PR
				3.04	Manchester	9A	RS
				3.32	Windermere	1B	RS
				4.00	Glasgow	5A	RS
				4.30	Kendal	5A	RS
				5.05	Glasgow	1B	RS
				5.24	Manchester	9A	RS
				5.57	Liverpool	8A	RS
				6.30	Holyhead	6J	RS
				6.50	Glasgow	12A	D
				7.03	Glasgow	1B	D
				7.13	Perth	1B	RS
				7.20	Glasgow	1B	D
7.55	Liverpool	1B	D				
				8.05	Stranraer	1B	RS
				8.20	Inverness	5A	D
8.30	Manchester	9A	RS				
8.50	Wolverhampton	1B	J				
9.00	Wolverhampton	3B	J				
9.45	Manchester	9A	RS				
				9.56	Wolverhampton	3B	J
10.00	Glasgow	1B	D				
				10.30	Wolverhampton	3B	J
10.40	Carlisle	1B	D				
10.50	Blackpool	1B	RS				
				11.09	Crewe	5A	D
				11.25	Manchester	9A	RS
				11.35	Heysham	1B	RS
11.45	Manchester	9A	RS				

Key to sheds:
1B Camden, 3B Bushbury, 5A Crewe, 6J Holyhead, 8A Edge Hill, 9A Longsight, 12A Carlisle Upperby (12 B 1948-1950) (12A1950-1958) (12B again 1958 -1966), 24E Blackpool

Key to loco classes:
D = Duchess, PR = Princess Royal, J = Jubilee, RS = Royal Scot
Britannia class locos were the most noticeable of all BR types with engines from both Manchester Longsight and Holyhead Sheds.

EUSTON AFTERNOON PRINCIPAL SERVICES

Departures   Arrivals

Departures				Arrivals			
				12.00	Liverpool	8A	PR
12.30	Liverpool	8A	PR				
				12.41	Wolverhampton	3B	J
				12.48	Manchester	9A	RS
12.50	Wolverhampton	3B	J				
				12.55	Blackpool	1B	RS
				13.05	Manchester	9A	RS
				13.20	Holyhead	6J	RS
13.30	Glasgow	5A	D	13.30	Wolverhampton	3B	J
13.35	Blackpool	24E	J				
				13.45	Liverpool	8A	PR
				13.55	Manchester	9A	RS
14.20	Wolverhampton	3B	J				
14.30	Liverpool	8A	RS	14.30	Wolverhampton	3B	J
14.45	Manchester	9A	RS	14.45	Liverpool	8A	J
15.00	Birmingham	1B	J				
				15.05	Blackpool	1B	J
				15.37	Llandudno	5A	J
15.45	Manchester	9A	J	15.45	Manchester	9A	J
				16.12	Carlisle	1B	D
16.30	Manchester	1B	RS				
				16.34	Wolverhampton	1B	J
16.37	Wolverhampton	3B	J				
16.55	Liverpool	8A	RS				
17.05	Blackpool	1B	RS				
				17.15	Glasgow	1B	D
17.35	Holyhead	5A	RS				
				17.45	Liverpool	8A	RS
17.50	Wolverhampton	3B	J				
				17.54	Manchester	9A	RS

The last year of traditional operations on the West Coast Main Line was 1959. By November schedules were eased to allow electrification work south of Crewe, and frequent delays and weekend diversions became the norm for unfortunate passengers. This continued for a long period as Euston Station was modernised.

EVENING EUSTON PRINCIPAL SERVICES

	Arrivals				Departures		
				18.00	Manchester	9A	RS
				18.10	Liverpool	8A	PR
				18.20	Heysham	1B	RS
18.30	Wolverhampton	1B	J	18.30	Preston	5A	D
				18.55	Wolverhampton	3B	J
				19.00	Birmingham	5A	RS
				19.20	Inverness	1B	RS
19.26	Perth	1B	D				
				19.30	Perth	1B	D
19.52	Manchester	9A	RS				
20.20	Liverpool	8A	RS				
				20.30	Glasgow (TPO)	5A	D
20.50	Liverpool	1B	D	20.50	Holyhead	6J	RS
21.00	Glasgow	1B	D				
				21.10	Glasgow	1B	D
21.20	Manchester	9A	RS				
				21.25	Glasgow	12A	D
				21.35	Birmingham	1B	J
				22.00	Manchester	9A	RS
				22.45	Manchester	9A	RS
				22.52	Perth	6J	RS
23.04	Blackpool	24E	J				
				23.05	Windermere	5A	J
				23.50	Glasgow	1B	RS

(TPO) is the Travelling Post Office, known to railwaymen as the West Coast Postal or The Night Mail.

In the late 1950s, relief trains were sometimes used on services when required. These generally departed ten minutes before the main train.

Country End Arrivals

For several decades schoolboys (some schoolgirls) and adults were seen at platform ends, observing the trains in a harmless pastime. Spotters had their favourite stations and favourite engines. At Euston the variety on show included all the Stanier 4-6-0 and 4-6-2 classes. 'Namers' galore!

Sightings over several days revealed many engines on the same workings. When locomotives had to be serviced, others from the same depot, normally of the same class, appeared. For the spotters this proved ideal as other names and numbers could be noted.

Although a Duchess was always a special sighting, the engines most eagerly awaited had to be the Princess Royal class. Two were based in Scotland; the others at Crewe and Liverpool. The approach into Euston of The Merseyside Express or The Red Rose normally gave a strong possibility of seeing one of the seven based at 8A Edge Hill.

For those who wanted more variety during a lull at Euston, just a short walk to King's Cross station gave sights of the Gresley A4s, known to spotters as 'Streaks'. As King's Cross was Eastern territory, most engines there had numbers that began with a '6', which required the Eastern Region version of Ian Allan's *abc* to note observations.

Re-built Patriot No. 45530, *Sir Frank Ree*, of 9A Longsight Shed, Manchester, has its name and number recorded by young spotters. Short trousers and navy gabardine coats and shed allocations date the view to 1959. *(R. S. Collection)*

Black Five No. 45004 brings in its train of non-corridor stock, passing under the bridge at Ampthill Square. On the platform trolley a lanky schoolboy wearing short trousers relaxes while number taking. *(Travel Lens Photographic)*

Young spotters reach for their pencils to record Jubilee No. 45592 *Indore* in either notebooks or a spotters' *abc* in May 1960. *(R .S. Collection)*

Re-built Royal Scot No. 46160 *Queen Victoria's Rifleman* of 9A Longsight Depot on the Up Mancunian from the then Manchester London Road arrives at Platform 1. *(R. S. Collection)*

One of the only two rebuilt Jubilees, No. 45736 *Phoenix* of 1B Camden Shed, enters Platform 2. Judging by his short jacket the sole observer is probably a signalman. *(R. S. Collection)*

The Mancunian approaches platform two, headed by a 9A Longsight-based Royal Scot, No. 46151 *The Royal Horse Guardsman*. Engine spotters were tolerated at Euston as the sign indicates; at some stations such as Tamworth, they were not welcome at all. *(R. S. Collection)*

On 1 August 1959 a Patriot in original form, No. 45538 *Giggleswick* of 1A Willesden Depot on what is probably an empty-stock train. Spotters on the left make themselves comfortable in the usual way, on a commandeered platform trolley. *(Gresley Society)*

Black Five No. 44860 arrives with a local train composed of non-corridor stock. The bracket on the smokebox is relocated from its original place over the handrail as a safety measure. Many locos received this modification due to imminent electrification clearance concerns 1964. *(A. G. Forsyth/Initial Photographics)*

Jubilee No. 45606, *Falkland Islands*, of 1B Camden Depot heads to Platform 1 to complete her journey. The name to spotters simply meant another 'Jub' at that time. *(R. S. Collection)*

The pioneer Deltic never gained a name or a number as it remained the property of its makers, English Electric. For a period in the 1950s it ran trials on The Merseyside Express where it proved very successful. As the London Midland Region had electrification plans the Deltic locos became replacements for Gresley A4s on the Eastern Region. *(Gresley Society)*

The Mancunian, at Platform 1 with Royal Scot No. 46114, *Coldstream Guardsman*. The engine was allocated to 8A Edge Hill Liverpool Depot. Observers are railway staff, a porter and signalman. *(R. K. Blencowe)*

Above: About 5 tons of coal has been used from the 9-ton capacity tender of No. 46170 *British Legion*. Youngsters cluster around to record a sighting while an adult obscures the nameplate from view. The engine was the star in the 1930s LMS film *Engine on Shed*. Since then the loco acquired a double chimney, smoke deflectors, straight steam pipes and a Stanier style cab. It was the only rebuilt Scot to have the LMS Crimson Lake livery. *(R. S. Collection)*

Right: The large ornate nameplate of No. 46170 *British Legion*. *(R. S. Collection)*

Un-named, as-built Patriot No. 45551 assists in backing out the stock of the arriving express train from Platform 1. The Patriot banked the train for the one mile over Camden Bank before going on shed at Camden. *(R. K. Blencowe)*

The Wolverhampton to Euston service was named The Midlander, and worked to two-hour timings for its 162 mile journey. Bushbury Depot 3B had an allocation of the later series Jubilees for this train. Jubilee No. 45741 *Leinster* arrives in Euston. *(Gresley Society)*

The Midlander observed once more, this train headed by another 3B Jubilee, No. 45734 *Meteor*. Engines from The Midlander often used the turntable at Euston for a fast turn-around; Camden Shed men would bring coal forward in the tender and top-up the water level. The gentleman with the case is a most likely a signalman going off duty. *(R. S. Collection)*

Jubilee No. 45741 *Leinster* arrives in Euston on another day; 3B Bushbury Shed took great pride in the appearance of engines for The Midlander. On Platform 2, the fireman of a Fowler tank engine couples up to remove empty coaching stock. *(Gresley Society)*

Royal Scot No. 46140 *The Kings Royal Rifle Corps* on The Mancunian is the next arrival after the Midlander. In 1956 three express services, the Royal Scot, Merseyside Express and Mancunian, received refurbished Mark 1 coaching stock painted in the region's colour choice of maroon with black and yellow lining. *(Gresley Society)*

Rebuilt Patriot No. 45545 *Planet*, a Crewe engine, heads into platform three. The coaches show variety in liveries. The 1950s 'Blood and Custard' on the Kitchen Car contrasts with the new maroon livery on the passenger stock. *(Gresley Society)*

One of the only two Princess class engines to survive after withdrawal, No. 46203 *Princess Margaret Rose*. The Shamrock originated at 8.10 a.m. from Liverpool Lime Street in conjunction with sailings to Belfast and Dublin. 8 May 1960. *(R. S. Collection)*

The station canopy above a nicely cleaned Royal Scot No. 46169, *The Boy Scout,* is in need of some maintenance, as indeed are other areas of 1950s Euston. *(R. S. Collection)*

Although Black Fives were numerous and popular with enginemen, spotters just wished they could be one of the four elusive named examples. Nicely lit with sunshine is No. 45395 of 3D Aston Depot. *(R. S. Collection)*

One of the early Black Fives built in 1935 by Vulcan Foundry with a combined top feed and dome. The parcels train is a Northampton working with No. 45091 of 2E Depot. *(Travel Lens Photographics)*

Royal Scot No. 46160, *Queen Victoria's Rifleman,* on The Mancunian is admired by two generations of enthusiasts. *(R. S. Collection)*

The enormous boiler of No. 46204 *Princess Louise* is seen to good advantage in this profile view of the loco entering Platform 2. *(G. Coltas)*

Light Engine and Shunting Movements

Vulcan Foundry-built Black Five No. 45088 backs onto her stock at Platform 13. *(Gresley Society) Below:* Fowler 2-6-4T No. 42367 brings empty stock into platform 14 in April 1962. *(B. W. L. Brooksbank/Initial Photographics)*

The driver of Patriot No. 45511, *Isle of Man*, seems happy with the world as he waits to head out of Euston. Although the original as-built Patriots looked dated they had a certain charm about them. *(R. S. Collection)*

Jubilee No. 45666 *Cornwallis*, a Crewe North loco, backs onto her train. Spotters poised in readiness for another arrival cluster alongside a Hughes /Fowler Crab on Platform 2. *(R. S. Collection)*

Two of Camden's Jinty Tank engines, No. 47514 and No. 47671, work Empty Stock about the station. *(Both Gresley Society)*

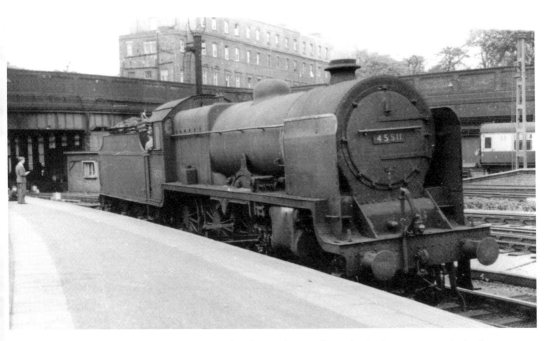

Willesden Shed's Patriot No. 45511, *Isle of Man*, having brought in the empty stock, backs out as light engine. Probably a summer working as the engine normally stayed coupled up by the buffer stops to provide heating until the train engine coupled up to the train, *c.* 1958. *(R. K. Blencowe)*

Black Five No. 44909 of 2A Rugby Shed backs out to travel to Camden to be turned, coaled up and watered. *(Gresley Society)*

A nicely cleaned 8F from Willesden Shed, No. 48624 moves empty stock. The engine was one of a small batch built at Ashford in 1943. The metal sign for Stephens Inks seemed to occupy many station walls on the railway system. *(Gresley Society)*

An immaculate Class 3 Fowler 2-6-2 tank engine, No. 40044 from Willesden Shed, prepares to remove empty-stock, *c.* 1958. The engines, like the Stanier version, were considered to be underpowered, but suited to menial tasks. *(R. K. Blencowe)*

Willesden's No. 78039. Riddles' well regarded and versatile design of 2-6-0, the class were all built at Darlington. In reality this BR standard version is an up-date of the 1946 LMS Ivatt engines. Among typical Euston clutter, carriage end boards can be seen in June 1963. *(D. Loveday)*

Another of Willesden's BR standards, No. 73004, is in a grimy condition on E.C.S. working, *c.* 1959. The Riddles design saw use throughout the whole network. *(R. K. Blencowe)*

A Stanier 8F, No. 48514 shows the grubby grey condition in which goods engines were often seen. The leading carriage is a twelve-wheel restaurant car. Crates on the trolleys are for the Railway Clearing House. The lorry is one of various makes and vintage always present at the end of Platform 1, and seen here on 19 September 1959. *(Gresley Society)*

A Stanier Jubilee, but paired with a Fowler 3,500 gallon tender, No. 45704 *Leviathan*, reverses out. In the background are the remains of the bridge removed in readiness for Euston's rebuilding. More than fifty years later travellers can still see the scars. 29 July 1964. *(Gresley Society)*

A Fowler tender has been fitted to No. 45721 *Impregnable* – no reasons are noted. Enginemen detested this version as its width was a lot less than the Stanier design and could prove hazardous. At one time the engine ran with tender from (LMS) No. 6100 *Royal Scot*, April 1963. *(D. Loveday)*

Jubilee No. 45721 *Impregnable* does a spell of shunting into the anything but agricultural area of Euston known as 'The Field'. The engine is now fitted with the Stanier version of tender. Evidence of the demise of Euston is seen in the background. *(R. S. Collection)*

Camden Jinty No. 47302 is pictured in profile as she moves empty-stock. The plate at the rear of the coal bunker gave a slight increase in coal capacity. What is of interest to the spotters will forever remain a mystery. *(R. S. Collection)*

A Hughes/Fowler Crab 2-6-0, one of the first LMS-designed engines, No. 42891 backs out light-engine under bridge No. 3, Ampthill Square, on 28 December 1959. *(Gresley Society)*

A Look Around

With no departures or arrivals expected, spotters wandered around the station. A check in the other platforms possibly revealed an engine from a parcels train, or one on station shunting duty. A look inside the Great Hall, or a visit to the buffet or possibly the bookstall, during a lull could fill in some time. Examination of the arrivals board kept them up to date with the next arrivals. No opportunity to see and record engine numbers would be missed.

In common with many stations Euston had places worth a look, hidden from view, and concealing an engine that spotters needed to underline in their *abcs*.

No. 46240 *City of Coventry* is somewhat of a mystery. Its location is the extremity of the departures platforms, but facing the wrong way. The lamps indicate a light-engine movement, possibly to use the hidden from view turntable alongside Platform 15. The ancient loco boiler at the side is one used for carriage heating, a sight seen at several stations throughout the system. *(Travel Lens Photographic)*

Surrounded by scaffolding, barriers and general clutter, No. 46239 *City of Chester* is in between Platforms 7 and 8. The bay where the coach is located appears to be a shortened platform. A distinct odour could be detected around this part of the station, due no doubt to loads inside some of the goods wagons that arrived in nearby sidings. *(Travel Lens Photographic)*

In the same location as seen previously, No. 46256 *Sir William A. Stanier F.R.S.*, the last-built LMS locomotive, on what is probably a parcels train. The crates are labelled Wolverton. *(Travel Lens Photographic)*

Buffer Stops

Most express steam locomotives were cleaned regularly. In Platform 3, No. 46236 *City of Bradford* is a credit to the cleaners of her Carlisle home depot in April 1962. *(D. Loveday)*
Below: Two Duchesses rest by the buffer stops of Platforms 1 and 2. Although only ten were named after Duchesses, spotters referred to the class as Semis or Duchesses. On view are Camden-based No. 46234 *Duchess of Abercorn* and the Scottish-based No. 46230 *Duchess of Buccleuch*, a name spotters had trouble in pronouncing. *(Peter Brock Archive/ Gresley Society)*

Pictured during her working days, No. 46235, *City of Birmingham,* is a green liveried example of the class. On withdrawal the engine found a home in a museum in the city of her name. *(Travel Lens Photographic)*

Occasionally a 2P 4-4-0 would be attached to a train when the weight limit was exceeded. Crewe-based No. 40660 has piloted an un-identified Scot or Patriot on The Ulster Express, *c.* 1958. Typical of Euston, in Platform 2, mail bags are piled ready for removal. *(R. K. Blencowe)*

One of the prized Camden locos always kept in a nice external condition, No. 46245 *City of London*. The engine became the first of several Pacifics to be painted in red in the late 1950s, a shade very similar to the LMS livery. *(Travel Lens Photographic)*

Newly arrived into Platform 3, No. 46228 *Duchess of Rutland*. A porter is unloading parcels from the coach behind the tender, while further down the platform yet more incoming parcels are piled high. *(Travel Lens Photographic)*

Class-leader No. 46200 *The Princess Royal* has brought in the oldest named train on the system,
The Irish Mail. Evidence of the diesel invasion are the two Class 40s (then numbered in D200
series) in Platforms 1 and 3. In the cab rank, passengers board the line of Austin FX3 taxis.
(R. S. Collection)

Lustre is given off a nice, clean No. 46225 *Duchess of Gloucester*. Unusually, Platform 1 is
uncluttered and the station nearly deserted in this photograph from April 1962. *(D. Loveday)*

Two of the Britannia-class locos named several years after they entered traffic. Both have the S. C. addition under their shedplates which shows they are fitted with self-cleaning smokeboxes. The Irish Mail engine became No. 70048, *The Territorial Army 1958*, in that year, while No. 70046 was named *Anzac* in September 1959. Photo *c*. 1958. *(R. K. Blencowe)*

Carlisle-based No. 46237, *City of Bristol*, draws to a stop in Platform 2. The release points which allowed locomotive removal if needed can be seen on Platform 1. August 1962. *(D. Loveday)*

The Ulster Express headed by No. 46247, *City of Liverpool,* is ex-Heysham. The Shamrock, in the charge of No. 46226, *Duchess of Norfolk,* is the 8.10 a.m. ex-Liverpool Lime Street. Both workings are from Irish boat sailings, *c.* 1958. *(R. K. Blencowe)*

Rebuilt Patriot No. 45540, *Sir Robert Turnbull,* waits to be cleared to go on-shed. Passengers have left the train and a few minutes will elapse as parcels are unloaded. In a short time a Willesden engine would couple up to remove the empty stock to the carriage sidings for cleaning. *(R. S. Collection)*

Activity all around No. 46246 *City of Manchester*. The ladies are certainly not passengers; possibly they are Clearing House staff. On Platform 2 a taxi driver, hands in pockets, waits for his next fare. Meanwhile the Pepsodent poster lady gives a smile. *(R. S. Collection)*

Express power from the Irish boat trains, No. 46256, *Sir William A. Stanier F.R.S.*, in Platform 2 with The Ulster Express. The Shamrock in Platform 1 has just arrived with No. 46208 *Princess Helena Victoria*. *(R. K. Blencowe)*

A double-header with two Black Fives. The crew of No. 45299 seem impatient to back the now empty stock out. The lead engine is 1E Bletchley based, probably put on to assist in April 1963. *(D. Loveday)*

Royal Scot No. 46148, *The Manchester Regiment*, deserves a second look from the passing schoolboy. The curve of the track and sweep of the roof canopy are seen to good effect. *(R. S. Collection)*

The Mancunian, ex-Manchester London Road, with rebuilt Patriot No. 45540 *Sir Robert Turnbull* of 9A Longsight Depot, seen in the 1950s. *(R. K. Blencowe)*

The Shamrock always provided a variety of motive power; today it's the turn of a Royal Scot, No. 46124 *London Scottish*. For the 8A Edge Hill footplate crew this was a lodging turn, *c.* 1958. *(R. K. Blencowe)*

Jubilee No. 45709 *Implacable,* at this time based at 3B Bushbury, with what is probably The Midlander from Wolverhampton, *c.* 1958. *(R. K. Blencowe)*

The train engine on this arrival is Patriot No. 45501 *St Dunstan's.* The nameplate could be described more as a badge, certainly a complete variation from the normal curved examples. 24 July 1959. *(R. K. Blencowe)*

The time is 8.28 a.m. and a few people are walking to work down Platform 1; parcels have been unloaded from the train. On Platform 2 a Royal Mail worker sorts through some incoming mail as his van occupies the taxi road. The engine, No. 46235 *City of Birmingham*, completes the scene; the train is most likely an arrival from Inverness or Stranraer. *(R. S. Collection)*

City gents take a glance at their train engine, No. 46225, *Duchess of Gloucester*, on what is probably an early arrival of The Irish Mail express. For a long period the advertisement on the clock was for the Phoenix Assurance Company. *(R. S. Collection)*

A few of the Britannia class were named some years after entering service, due to some having Westinghouse brake equipment fitted. As smoke deflectors were initially not fitted to both No. 70043 and No. 70044, there was nowhere to mount the nameplate. Now with deflectors and nameplate fitted; No. 70044 *Earl Haig* has travelled from Manchester with The Mancunian. The other late naming was No. 70043, *Lord Kitchener, c.* 1958. *(R. K. Blencowe)*

The guard looks out to see how soon before No. 46168 *The Girl Guide* is ready to move out as its driver boards the footplate. Occasionally train crews might receive instructions to travel home, 'on the cushions' and Willesden or Camden men took over. *(R. S. Collection)*

Much activity surrounds No. 46220 *Coronation*. While the business of unloading goes on, the driver, fireman and guard use the time with a conversation, April 1962. *(D. Loveday)*

The footplate crew of red-liveried No. 46248, *City of Leeds*, check progress with parcels unloading. The lamp code has been changed and they await permission to reverse up the bank to Camden Shed. *(R. S. Collection)*

A lunchtime arrival could possibly be one from Blackpool due to arrive at 12.55 p.m. A Watford commuter electric train is in the next platform alongside No. 46209 *Princess Beatrice*. *(R. S. Collection)*

A sleeper train arrives at 8.29 a.m. headed by No. 46220 *Coronation*. Two ladies await another arrival of probably another of the sleepers due in Platform 2. The bases of the roof support columns are inserts placed under the original pillars to raise the roof by six feet, an alteration required to increase ventilation of the area. *(R. S. Collection)*

Royal Scot No. 46150, *The Life Guardsman,* of 6J Holyhead pulls to a halt with the Irish Mail. Unusually, the train headboard has been placed above the buffer beam. *(R. S. Collection)*

In the time honoured tradition, a father shows his son under the engine, No. 46229 *Duchess of Hamilton.* A porter takes care of luggage while passengers mill around the driver. In Platform 1, No. 46131, *The Royal Warwickshire Regiment,* has arrived from Manchester.

Gordon Coltas probably travelled on the Royal Scot-headed train to a meeting in London; he explained that he always took his camera along. *(Gordon Coltas).*

The headlamp has somehow remained in position despite it leaning at a precarious angle on No. 46206, *Princess Marie Louise*, on 28 December 1959. *(Gresley Society)*

The ominous signs of change; the buffer stops have been moved and scaffolding supports suggest the destruction of Euston is about to commence. A change also to rebuilt Patriot No. 45539 *Sir Frank Ree* of 1A Willesden; the lamp bracket on the smokebox has been re-located ready for working under electrified lines. *(R. S. Collection)*

A red-liveried No. 46238 *City of Carlisle,* having stopped for a period of time, has her cylinder drain valves opened before backing out. On Platform 1, railway workers are going to, and some returning from, work – probably in the Railway Clearing House. *(Travel Lens Photographic)*

The crew of Carlisle-based No. 46236 *City of Bradford* watch the progress of unloading parcels. Alongside Platform 2 a chauffeur waits by his car, which is parked in readiness for the next train. *(Travel Lens Photographic)*

Scottish-based No. 46231 *Duchess of Atholl* eases cautiously toward the buffers in Platform 1. A 10 m.p.h. restriction was placed over points and crossings on arriving trains. In March 1953 Patriot No. 45514 *Holyhead* approached too quickly and hit the buffers. *(Travel Lens Photographic)*

Rugby 2A-based Black Five No. 44870 double-heads an un-identified Britannia. Both engines show a good head of steam; possibly the reason for double-heading could be a train over the weight limit. *(Travel Lens Photographic)*

Carlisle 12B-based No. 46237 *City of Bristol*. On Platform 2 the taxis line up ready for fares. On Platform 1 there are quite a variety of railway vehicles. August 1962. *(D. Loveday)*

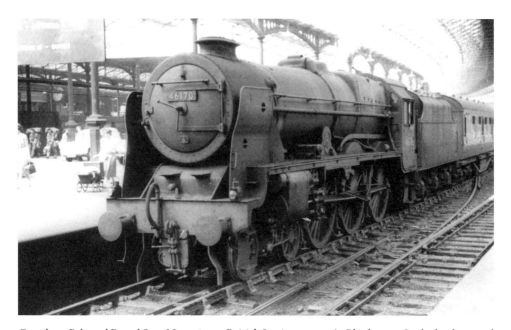

Camden 1B-based Royal Scot No. 46170, *British Legion*, at rest in Platform 2. In the background two soldiers, possibly National Servicemen, are loaded up with kit bags and cases. It is hoped that a child is not under the suitcase the two ladies with the pram are pushing. 24 July 1959. *(R. K. Blencowe)*

The fireman of Longsight 9A-based Royal Scot No. 46111, *Royal Fusilier,* having changed the headlamp code, talks to the guard as the train is unloaded. *(R. S. Collection)*

Jubilee No. 45681 *Aboukir* pushes coaching stock out of Platform 2. On Platform 1 there is evidence of a parcel splitting open, and at the far end platform trolleys are in abundance alongside a variety of road vehicles. *(R. S. Collection)*

Liverpool 8A Edge Hill-based No. 46200 *The Princess Royal* stands alongside one of the LMS diesel twins, either 10000 or 10001. The Princess is in maroon livery. *(R. S. Collection)*

It is 8.32 a.m. and the familiar procession make their way to work again. The fireman has changed the lamps on No. 46250 *City of Lichfield* ready to back down to Camden Shed. Two arrivals expected in at this time were from Inverness and Stranraer. *(R. S. Collection)*

The Royal Scot with several differences. The only obvious one is the Stanier type of cab, but No. 46170 *British Legion* had a non-standard boiler to the rest of the class. The engine was a rebuild of the ill-fated LMS No. 6399 *Fury* in 1935. *(R. S. Collection)*

One of the 8A Edge Hill members of the class, No. 46208, *Princess Helena Victoria,* in red livery waits to back out of Platform 1. The Scammell Scarab has the chequers on its body-side to indicate inter-station parcels traffic. *(Gresley Society)*

Double-heading with Royal Scots was comparatively rare. On this occasion a very grimy example, No. 46131, *Royal Warwickshire Regiment,* of 6G Llandudno Junction Shed has piloted an un-identified member of the same class. Number 46131 was transferred from 9A Longsight to 6G in March 1962. *(R. S. Collection)*

Crewe-based No. 46235 *City of Birmingham,* probably on an arrival of the Inverness sleeper train, blows steam from the cylinders in readiness to bank her Empty-Stock up Camden bank. *(R. S. Collection)*

Carlisle-based Royal Scot No. 46122 *Royal Ulster Rifleman* stands alongside the Deltic-bodied DP2 diesel. The Scot's driver and fireman peer out of the cab to see the tractor tow a rake of platform trolleys ready to unload the train. *(R. S. Collection)*

The whole atmosphere of the old Euston is captured as Royal Scot No. 46111 *Royal Fusilier* brings in The Mancunian. The sweeping platform and curvature of the roof with its herringbone effect are shown to give a good diorama of what was swept away in later days. The engine is not the main feature, but the people clustered on Platform 2 and other forms of transport are. *(Gresley Society)*

To Camden Shed for Servicing

When an up-train arrived in Euston, loco spotters recorded the event in their notebooks or the Ian Allan *ABC*. They stopped to admire the loco for a short time at the buffer stops, their requests to the driver to climb on the footplate refused as too many officials would be around. Passengers quite often thanked the driver for a punctual arrival and sometimes passed him their newspapers.

Within minutes the platform swarmed with activity. Passengers spilled out of the coaches and porters appeared to take charge of luggage (as efficiently as possible so as to generate tips). Soon the area became littered with parcels, trolleys, and sack trucks.

Incoming passengers headed for the nearest exit or over to Platform 2 where a line of taxis waited to take them onwards. Meanwhile, porters began unloading a huge amount of packages onto platform trolleys, readying their transportation to the Parcels Office on Platform 1 prior to sorting and despatch to their destinations.

Passengers disembarked, parcels unloaded, the Platform Inspector advised the loco crew. The train engine then uncoupled, yet remained buffered up to the coaches. A 1A Willesden loco removed the empty stock to the carriage cleaning depot, banking assistance up Camden Bank provided by the train engine. At Camden depot, the train engine fell away for its crew to gain access to the shed. The loco then turned on the turntable, a disposal crew taking over while the driver and fireman booked off-shift.

Before leaving, the driver filled in the journey log, citing reasons for any delays. Both driver and guard compared logs prior to handing them in at the shed office, reporting any engine faults that needed attention.

Light Engine Movements
on Camden Bank

Nicely cleaned Jubilee No. 45669 *Fisher* of 2B Nuneaton Shed backs down to Camden Shed in July 1962. *(D. Loveday)*

Motive power for The Lakes Express is rebuilt Royal Scot No. 46167, *The Hertfordshire Regiment.* July 1962. *(D. Loveday)*

Stanier Black Five No. 45271 falls back from the express she has just banked over the Camden Gradients, in June 1963. *(D. Loveday)*

One of the powerful and sprightly Stanier 2-6-4 tank engines, No. 42606, in June 1963. *(D. Loveday)*

A Fowler version of the 2-6-4 tank engine, No. 42367 of 1A Willesden was regarded as one of the best of Willesden's allocation. The cleanliness of the engine is noticeable, as photographed in July 1962. *(D. Loveday)*

Primrose Hill Tunnel

Just a short distance beyond Camden loco shed – as the line curves westwards – you will find the delightfully named Primrose Hill Tunnel. One of the most ornate practical structures on the line, it was completed in 1837 and expanded in 1879 when a second portal was added. The tunnel was built in order to satisfy the demands of landowners, the Chalcot Estate. Its stonework portals are very impressive, although passengers have little chance to admire their grandeur due to the curvature of the track and the high wall at trackside. Photographers also found difficulty accessing the location safely.

The superb architecture forms a backdrop to Black Five No. 45385 of 3B Bescot Shed. The train of empty coaching stock of The Lakes Express emerges from the tunnel. *(Peter Brock Archive/ Gresley Society)*

With chrome-plated nameplate and cab-side numbers, class leader No. 45552 *Silver Jubilee* exits the tunnel. In reality No. 45552 is No. 45642 *Boscawen*, as their identities were swapped in 1935, when a special gloss exhibition-finish black livery with chromed boiler bands was applied to the engine. *(Peter Brock Archive/Gresley Society)*

Judging by the exhausts from her double chimney, Royal Scot No. 46150 *The Life Guardsman* of 5A Crewe North Shed is steaming well as she hurries a down train along. *(Peter Brock Archive/ Gresley Society)*

Camden Bank

Down departures normally had assistance up Camden Bank for one mile from the loco which had brought in the train as empty-stock banking at the rear. One of the ex-streamliners, No. 46221 *Queen Elizabeth*, pulls out of Euston at the start of the incline. *(Peter Brock Archive/ Gresley Society)*

Same engine but on a different day; No. 46221 *Queen Elizabeth* is pictured this time in July 1962 with a different train. (The previous picture showed a General Utility Van in the formation.) *(D. Loveday)*

The down Merseyside Express hauled by No. 46236, *City of Bradford,* has just cleared the Camden Goods Depot on the left. A normal load for The Merseyside express was often fifteen overcrowded coaches. The footbridge in the background led from the engine shed to the goods depot. April 1962. *(D. Loveday)*

The ultimate shot photographers dreamed of: a Princess, No. 46206 *Princess Marie Louise,* on an up train passes No. 46248 *City of Leeds* in July 1962. To quote David Loveday, 'I remember taking those photos, the sight and smell and sound were terrific. Waiting on Camden bank for four consecutive steam hauled expresses. They were in the minority then.' *(D. Loveday)*

Seen at close quarters, rebuilt Patriot No. 45529 *Stephenson* of 1A Willesden passes Camden Shed in June 1963. It would prove very noisy as the engine appears to be working hard. Drivers needed to take care not to task too much out of the engine so soon after departure, as the thirty miles to Tring is nearly all uphill. *(D. Loveday)*

Rebuilt Patriot No. 45531, *Sir Frederick Harrison*, of 8A Edge Hill Liverpool, passes an early design diesel which is entering Camden Shed, April 1962. *(D. Loveday)*

At the top of the bank just before reaching Camden Shed, No. 46254 *City of Stoke-on-Trent*. The small badge above the nameplate is the coat of arms of the city. June 1963. *(D. Loveday)*

Green-liveried No. 46209 *Princess Beatrice* passes Camden loco shed. Camden goods depot is on the left, April 1962. *(D. Loveday)*

The last locomotive built by the LMS was named after the company Chief Mechanical Engineer, No. 46256 *Sir William A. Stanier F.R.S.* Stanier was responsible for the introduction of many successful LMS designs. The engine was the last of the class to be withdrawn. Photographed in July 1962. *(D. Loveday)*

An up-train headed by Britannia class No. 70018, *Flying Dutchman,* is just a few hundred yards from completing her journey. *(Peter Brock Archive/Gresley Society)*

The down Lakes Express with Royal Scot No. 46167, *The Hertfordshire Regiment,* passing an early diesel loco in July 1962. *(D. Loveday)*

Royal Scot No. 46169 *The Boy Scout* on a down express, probably to Manchester as 9A Longsight was her home depot. July 1962. *(D. Loveday)*

Red-liveried No. 46240 *City of Coventry*, a long term 1B Camden loco, is approaching her home depot in July 1962. *(D. Loveday)*

An up-train headed by No. 46206 *Princess Marie Louise* passes the original Camden Depot. This became the Roundhouse Theatre. April 1962. *(D. Loveday)*

Black Five No. 45050 pilots an unidentified Duchess on a down-express. It was unusual for a Pacific to require a pilot engine. The Black Five is probably only working back to Northampton, where she was based at 2E Depot. At times pilots were attached to up-trains having steaming problems. *(D. Loveday)*

The 18.50 Euston to Wolverhampton express, titled The Midlander, is headed by Jubilee No. 45741 *Leinster* on 18 July 1953. *(B. W. L. Brooksbank/ Initial Photographics)*

The gradient of Camden Bank is apparent as Patriot No. 45510, an un-named member of the class, passes under the footbridge that linked the goods depot to the loco shed. July 1949. *(R. K. Blencowe)*

Camden Motive Power Depot, coded 1B

An 1847 built shed replaced the initial one on the up-side of the line. The original engine shed on the up-side still exists as a Grade II listed building known as The Roundhouse Theatre. Although twenty-four locomotives could be housed around its 160-foot diameter, it soon became too small to suit the expansion of traffic. The replacement Camden Motive Power Depot lay one mile from Euston, on the down side by the crest of Camden Bank. Although small in comparison to other important sheds, Camden provided express locomotives for all principle workings from Euston.

The 1B Camden allocation for 1959 totalled forty-one locomotives, mostly express types – four Patriots, eight Jubilees, nine Royal Scots, eight Coronation Pacifics – whereas twelve Jinty Tank Engines featured for minor duties. Diesels arrived in the late 1950s.

The shed closed on 9 September 1963 when the remaining Camden locos transferred to 1A Willesden.

CAMDEN SHED LAYOUT

North   **

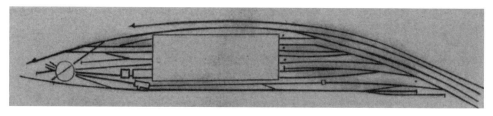

< To Willesden   To Euston >

As can be seen from the shed layout, 1B Camden was not large considering its allocation of locomotives numbered fifty-six in 1950, reducing to forty-one steam engines plus several diesels by 1959. This number ignores the arrivals on express trains from outposts of the West Coast Main Line.

Reversing from Euston up Camden Bank, entry to the shed was achieved by passing over the points at ** on the plan above. The loco moved onto the Cowans

Sheldon vacuum-operated turntable at the depot's north end. Turning using a vacuum provided by the locomotive, the turntable's motor took about one and a half minutes to complete the 180 degree turn. On completion of the turn, engines faced the correct direction for their next departure. They then progressed through the various stages of disposal, maintenance and preparation for future departures. Visiting engines always took priority for servicing over Camden's own allocation.

Proceeding through the shed yard, engines took on water, and had their fires cleaned under the ash plant. Loco tenders topped up with coal at one of the two 150-ton capacity coaling stages. The coal and 25-ton ash plants were both constructed c. 1937 by the Henry Lees Company.

Situated inside the shed lobby, the daily arrangements displayed on a chalked board indicated all the locations of engines on-shed, and their next destinations. Drivers checked times of departure for their engines and any restriction notices when booking on. In a throwback to pre-nationalisation days the engine's number had the '4' removed from its full number, so it was still known as in its LMS days. Any problems with that engine simply meant the footplate crew took the most convenient one down the order.

Through the 1950s manpower problems increased as work on-shed was considered both a dirty job and very poorly paid. At one time Camden employed thirty-two cleaners to keep its engines reasonably clean, but as time went by the cleanliness of 1B locos worsened. However, the pride in having a 1B engine on a royal train when required could still provide two sparkling clean Pacifics, one for the train, the other as a stand-by. Some engines were required to be set aside for inspection, or periodic boiler wash-outs. Others needed 'Not to Be Moved' signs placed on them while the cleaners set to work.

For years the lines of Royal Scots, Jubilees, and Duchesses remained the most common sight at the north end of the shed. The express engines all faced north, awaiting the time to back down the bank and couple up with their trains in Euston.

At the south end of the shed many more engines lined up for servicing ready for their next northbound turns of duty. For arriving loco crews on double-home turns, it required a walk to the nearby ninety-bed lodging quarters known as the 'Barracks'. The reputation of being the noisiest on the system, due to the train movements, proved to be true with sleep constantly disturbed by the passing trains. A former engineman recalled that he consumed several alcoholic nightcaps when in London to induce a better night of sleep.

Before coming off-shed, the loco's fireman made a trip to the stores to collect his tools, detonators, spare gauge glass, and sand to fill the sand boxes, also a headboard for the engine. Nearly all departures from Camden were named trains, and the aluminium headboards such as The Royal Scot, The Mancunian and The Caledonian had to be fixed above the smoke-box door. A tradition on Remembrance Day, maintained on the eleventh day of November, was the fixing of poppies around the smokebox of some departing engines.

Crews booked on well before departure time to inspect the entire engine before commencing oiling and sand box filling. The last duty of the fireman before the engine came off-shed was to brew up the tea for consuming on the trip.

All express engines departed off-shed in reverse gear to Euston, several engines backing down on most occasions to save line occupation. On reaching Euston they separated, signals directing them into their allocated platforms to couple ahead of their respective stock ready for departures.

A narrow pedestrian gateway in Dumpton Place, situated just off the Gloucester Road, gave entrance to 1B Camden Shed. For those with shed permits this was easy, but for those without official permission it proved difficult. David Loveday, who took many of the photographs in this book, explained that he simply walked in accompanied by a friend who worked at the shed. A simple but very effective way as his pictures testify.

The North End of Camden Shed

A scene so typical of each day at Camden: a Duchess, Royal Scot and Britannia face north in readiness for their next Euston train departures. The Jinty tank engine is only on shed to be coaled up or do shunting. The tender belongs to a Stanier design loco, reversed down-line after working its train into Euston. This loco will move over the points and on to shed via the turntable at the entrance to the shed yard. *(R. S. Collection)*

Scenes Around Camden's Turntable

City of Manchester No. 46246. The engine was formerly streamlined. When rebuilt, the chamfered smokebox remained. This chamfer proved the origin of the spotter's nickname of 'Semi' as they believed the engines to be semi-streamlined. In 1960 it became the last of the class to receive a full round version. July 1962. *(D. Loveday)*

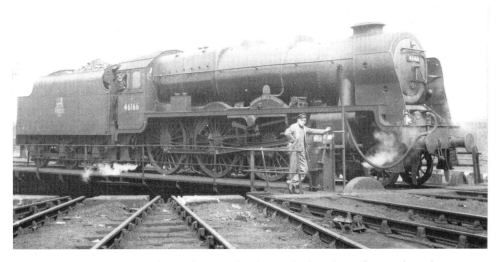

Royal Scot No. 46166, *London Rifle Brigade*. The tender has the early British Railways crest. Once connected to the vacuum motor, it took about one and a half minutes to complete the change of direction. *(R. S. Collection)*

The driver of Royal Scot No. 46157, *The Royal Artilleryman,* keeps a watchful eye on his fireman as the engine is turned using the turntable's vacuum motor. The crest on the tender is the late 1950s version. *(Gresley Society)*

Royal Scot No. 46140, *The King's Royal Rifle Corps,* has just been turned after entering the shed yard. The fireman hangs on in the traditional manner, both feet on the bottom step with a hold on the running plate handrail, on 15 June 1957. *(R. K. Blencowe)*

Camden's own engine, Jubilee No. 45592, *Indore*, in 1959. Engines from other sheds always received priority in servicing to have them ready for their return trips. *(R. K. Blencowe)*

Princess Royal class No. 46204, *Princess Louise,* turns on shed having just backed down from Euston after her arrival on The Merseyside Express, on 15 June 1957. *(R. K. Blencowe)*

Royal Scot No. 46131, *The Royal Warwickshire Regiment,* turns after arriving with The Mancunian. In the background a Princess-class loco awaits its turn for the table to become available, 27 October 1956. *(R. S. Collection)*

Clearing the table, No. 46234 *Duchess of Abercorn* will proceed through the shed together with the other recently arrived engine for routine checks and maintenance ready for its next departure. *(D. Loveday)*

Access to the coaling plant was only via the turntable road; No. 46221 *Queen Elizabeth* passes under the stage to have her 10-ton coal capacity tender topped up. The girder framework is to support the shed's water tank. *(D. Loveday)*

The next loco to go under the coaling plant is No. 46226 *Duchess of Norfolk*. The engine shows a 12A shedplate which indicates Carlisle Upperby as its home-base. Upperby Shed was recoded several times, fluctuating between 12A and 12B. April 1962. *(D. Loveday)*

Just five months before her withdrawal in September 1962, Camden Shed's own No. 46209 *Princess Beatrice*. The mineral wagon's content is coke, mixed into the coal bunkers to reduce the smoke pollution of engines on-shed. *(D. Loveday)*

Now coaled up ready for her next trip, No. 46221 *Queen Elizabeth* will back through towards the ash plant. *(D. Loveday)*

Passing through the line from the coal stage, No. 46220 *Coronation*, a one time record breaker with a speed of 114 mph, photographed in April 1962. *(D. Loveday)*

Camden Drivers

By the 1950s the high-speed runs of yesteryear, when a driver achieved a record, were a thing of the past. The two exceptions were up-trains from Carlisle with a newly introduced lightly loaded working named The Caledonian.

On 7 August 1957 the up-train with No. 46229 *Duchess of Hamilton* in the hands of Camden driver Bill Starvis and Fireman Wills arrived in Euston eleven minutes early. On 5 September 1957 Driver Starvis and Fireman Tumilty brought No. 46244 *King George VI* into Euston an amazing thirty-seven minutes early. The event attracted much needed positive publicity in the press and Bill Starvis featured in a televised interview. A congratulations letter to the crew followed shortly afterwards. It has to be said that The Caledonian was an easy task for a Pacific but for the engine to reach 96 m.p.h. with a normal working showed just how good both engine and crew were.

Although the name Bill Starvis appears in records for high speed runs, 1B Camden had other top-link drivers who never achieved the headlines. These included Camden men Steveson, Stoneman, Mounslow, Adderman, Thorpe, Evans, Barker, Pile, Wallace, Higgins, Mutch, Shepherd, Prior, Trowel, and Ireson (apologies for any omissions).

Ash pan cleaning is in progress alongside the Camden ash plant. Liverpool Edge Hill 8A-based No. 46243, *City of Lancaster,* has her fire-grate cleaned. *(D. Loveday)*

Motive power for The Welshman, No. 46238, *City of Carlisle,* of Carlisle Upperby Shed, will probably come off the train at Crewe. The Welshman was a summer-only express that ran between London Euston–Holyhead–Portmadoc–Pwllheli. Introduced in 1951, the titled train made its last run in August 1963. Photograph taken in July 1962. *(D. Loveday)*

Carlisle-based No. 46252, *City of Leicester,* stands over the ash pits alongside the ash plant. Unusually the express code headlamps are still in place on the buffer beam, in July 1962. *(D. Loveday)*

Now fitted with the headboard, The Royal Highlander, but awaiting headlamp coding is No. 46252, *City of Leicester*, in July 1962. The loco is ready to back down to Euston. The time of departure for The Royal Highlander sleeper-train to Inverness is 19.20. July 1962. *(D. Loveday)*

By July 1962, when this photograph was taken, the Camden allocation of Jinty tank engines had been displaced by Ivatt's design of the 2-6-2T. No. 41239 joins in the company of mainline express locos No. 46252 and Royal Scot No. 46169 *The Boy Scout*. *(D. Loveday)*

City of Chester, No. 46239, has lost its 1B shed plate, removed possibly in readiness for an imminent transfer to 6J Holyhead. The smoke from the tub shows the fire has been thrown out of the fire-box. June 1963. *(D. Loveday)*

Surrounded by the ever increasing number of diesels, Royal Scot No. 46162 *Queen's Westminster Rifleman* of 12 Carlisle Upperby Shed stands ahead of No. 46246 *City of Manchester*. *(R. S. Collection)*

Standing alongside one of the shed's diesel newcomers, No. 46246 *City of Manchester*. The shine given by the lighting off the paintwork shows the engine has been cleaned to a high standard. At one stage Camden employed thirty-two cleaners. Like similar engine sheds it later had problems in recruiting men for such dirty work. April 1962. *(D. Loveday)*

Inside the shed and positioned over an inspection pit, No. 46206 *Princess Marie Louise*. The shed plate has been removed and ash needs cleaning from under the smokebox. Presumably the engine was still in service as normally withdrawn locos were stored outside with their chimneys covered over. The Princess was withdrawn from Camden in November 1962 and later scrapped at Crewe Works. *(D. Loveday)*

Further along the shed, the Royal Scot that differed from its classmates, No. 46170 *British Legion.* One difference on the Stanier type cab side is noticeable, though the engine's slightly longer boiler is not apparent. April 1962. *(D. Loveday)*

Royal Trains

Royal workings originating from Euston were always a job for a Camden Duchess, code-named 'The Grove.' Details of such workings had to be carefully planned, with two Pacific locos cleaned to perfection as this was prestigious work. Two engines were prepared to ensure against an engine failure. The allocated loco had its buffers and drawbar hook removed and replaced with a special burnished set provided by Crewe Works. The other cleaned Pacific was kept on stand-by, just in case of problems.

For the driver and fireman a new set of overalls was issued for the occasion. Prior to the working, a 1B loco journeyed to Wolverton earlier in the day to pick up the royal train stock in readiness for the working. When not required the coaching stock was stabled at Wolverton. On the day the train always commenced its journey from Platform 6.

To drive a royal train, which demanded a four headlamp code, was a special event for both driver and fireman. Afterwards a small bonus payment was paid to the crew together with a letter of thanks from management. Whether royalty ever saw the engine or its crew has never been recorded.

The cleaning crew set to work to bring the appearance of No. 46240 *City of Coventry* up to the immaculate standard required for a royal train engine. The special cylinder covers are now fitted and receive a final wipe over. On the sack truck one of the burnished buffers awaits attaching to the buffer beam. Immediately behind No. 46240 is the selected stand-by engine, awaiting the attention of the cleaning gang after completing *City of Coventry;* its identity is unknown.

Willesden Shed also entered the spirit of royal workings and provided a sparkling clean loco into Euston (a Fowler 2-6-4 tank, No. 42350, noted in October 1962) with the empty coaching stock. It remained coupled up to provide steam heating until the train engine coupled up. July 1962. *(D. Loveday)*

The high shine given from the boiler cladding indicates the pride in the royal working. The cleaner's bucket would have a special solution for the task, or maybe just paraffin, photographed in July 1962. *(D. Loveday)*

On 8 January 1958, Camden driver Starvis and fireman Wills took No. 46245, *City of London,* to Euston for official inspection. The engine became the first of several Stanier Pacifics to receive a maroon livery and new BR logo. Another Pacific, No. 46250 *City of Lichfield,* also on display that day, exhibited the logo on a green liveried engine. Camden always kept No. 46245 in immaculate condition, as she was considered one of its best. The other favourite was No. 46244 *King George VI.* 6 July 1963. *(D. Loveday)*

Longsight Shed-based Royal Scot No. 46158, *The Loyal Regiment,* shows signs of a severe impact to her buffer beam. What caused the damage is unrecorded. 7 July 1962. *(D. Loveday)*

Two views of Crewe North 5A-based Jubilee No. 45721 *Impregnable*, taken in April 1963. *(D. Loveday)*

Jubilee No. 45705 *Seahorse*, at this time the pride of 24E Blackpool Shed. In later years she became a star performer on the Buxton to Manchester businessmen's train, seen here in June 1963. *(D. Loveday)*

The last-built LMS engine, No. 46256, *Sir William A. Stanier F.R.S.*, in maroon livery. Also on view is green-liveried No. 46235 *City of Birmingham* in June 1963. *(D. Loveday)*

With her chimney covered over while awaiting the decision on her future, No. 46207 *Princess Arthur of Connaught*. (Many wrongly thought her name should be Prince). A lesser engine, one of the powerful Hughes/Fowler Crab 2-6-0 locos, No. 42747, is still active as the steam around the cylinders shows. *(D. Loveday)*

Working through the back of shed road, No. 46238 *City of Carlisle*. The Carlisle Upperby-based loco sports the later smaller double-lined version of The Caledonian headboard. The reduced size was intended for use on diesel locos. Great speculation surrounded the future of No. 46238 as possibly a candidate for preservation in Carlisle. July 1962. *(D. Loveday)*

Prepared ready for its next departure back to Liverpool, is a very grimy No. 46208 *Princess Helena Victoria*. 8A Edge Hill allocated from 1951 until her withdrawal in October 1962. Unfortunately, when the loco received her red livery in the Crewe paint shop a mistake lead to orange and black lining being applied instead of the correct yellow and black colours. *(D. Loveday)*

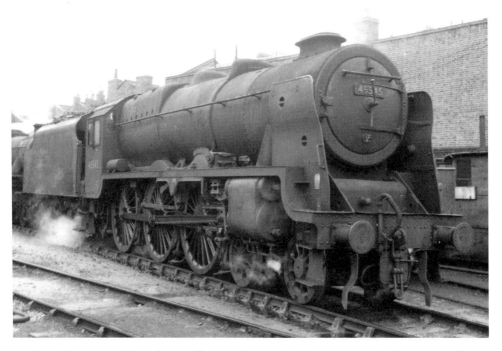

Looking like a Royal Scot, but really one of the rebuilt Patriots, this is No. 45545 *Planet*. Noticeable differences are Stanier type cab sides, and the absence of footholds above the buffer beam. *(D. Loveday)*

Express power old and new: No. 46252 *City of Leicester* and D223, later named *Lancastria*. The tender of No. 46252 is piled high with coal, far more than the 10-ton supposed capacity. *(Travel Lens Photographic)*

Royal Scot No. 46169, *The Boy Scout*, lined up behind another Scot. On the cab side a bracket intended to display the driver's name is seen just above the loco's number. *(D. Loveday)*

Backing down past the coaling plant in April 1962, Jubilee No. 45660 *Rooke* is commendably clean. The Britannia on the next line is No. 70033, *Charles Dickens,* of 9A Longsight Shed. *(D. Loveday)*

The cylinder drain cocks are opened in readiness to move off-shed on No. 46256, *Sir William A. Stanier F.R.S.* Based at 5A Crewe North, the loco is in need of attention by the cleaners on her return to Crewe. *(R. S. Collection)*

One nameplate is now on display at the National Railway Museum. Unfortunately, someone has machined the surface using the wrong speed and feed on a milling machine, evidenced by the circular grooves across the letters.

A Royal Scot with the most elaborate nameplate of all the ex-LMS engines, No. 46127 *Old Contemptibles*. The name commemorates the efforts of the British Expeditionary Force in the First World War. The German Kaiser had called them 'the Contemptible Little Army'. Like many other engines, No. 46127 had a speedometer fitted (shown on the rear wheel) after many years without one. Photograph *c.* 1959. *(D. Loveday)*

Author's own replica.

Probably due to the coke/coal mixture at Camden, Rugby 2A Shed's Jubilee No. 45670, *Howard of Effingham,* shows a clean exhaust in April 1962. *(D. Loveday)*

Having her tender topped up with water from the column, No. 46234 *Duchess of Abercorn.* The tender will take about five minutes to fill. July 1962. *(D. Loveday)*

The first-built LMS Pacific, No. 46200, *The Princess Royal*. Still in her Brunswick green livery, but in common with three others in the class will soon receive a maroon livery. Black Five No. 45259 stands alongside, photographed in 1958. *(D. Loveday)*

Nuneaton 2B-based Jubilee No. 45669 *Fisher* simmers during the late afternoon. She is awaiting the time to back down to Euston for The Highlander sleeper-train departure, July 1962. *(D. Loveday)*

The unique 4-6-2, No. 71000, *Duke of Gloucester*. Classed as 8P, the engine has Caprotti valve gear.

For most of her days she headed The Mid-Day Scot, on which the loco gained a bad reputation. As the working to Crewe is only 158 miles, the high pile of coal indicates one major problem.

Laid up at Crewe on withdrawal, after some considerable time there, a cylinder removed from the loco went for exhibition at the Science Museum. The engine eventually was sold for scrap. Fortunately a preservation society purchased No. 71000 and removed it from the scrapyard in South Wales to the Great Central Railway at Loughborough.

For years volunteers raised funds and restoration gradually took place, although a replacement cylinder had to be manufactured abroad at great cost.

Many years after withdrawal No. 71000 became a mainline engine once more, its BR days problems of erratic steaming now corrected. A new ash pan replaced the original one manufactured to the wrong dimensions.

In preservation the loco has lived up to the expectations that it promised and never achieved during her BR career. *(D. Loveday)*

Royal Scot No. 46166. The close proximity to residential properties is evident, which proved noisy when coal bunkers filled. Ash from the mechanical plant discharged into the line of wagons to be taken for disposal. *(R.S. Collection)*

Patriot No. 45546 *Fleetwood* stands behind another engine of the Patriot class at the rear of the engine shed. *(R. S. Collection)*

The final LMS engine, built shortly before nationalisation at Crewe Works. Showing the Ivatt modifications of the delta truck, and shortened cab sides No. 46256, *Sir William A. Stanier F.R.S.* really was a sight the spotters wished to see. Not normally noticed, are the round buffers on the tender, which suggests that Pacific locomotives' oval buffers were for cosmetic effect. In the background, Camden Goods Depot forms a backdrop in this image from July 1962. *(D. Loveday)*

Opposite the Camden loco shed on the up-side of the mainline stood the large extremely busy goods depot.

Until 1962 railways were obliged to carry anything at a fixed price based on weight because of the Common Carrier Act. The road haulage companies inspected the set railway charges then undercut the fixed weight tariff, leaving the railways with totally uneconomic loads of empty crates, etc. Goods traffic in later years became severely affected by increased road transport, and never recovered the enormous loss in business.

An un-named Patriot, No. 45513, stands ready to back down to Euston. The year is 1948 and the engine is finished in early BR black livery with maroon and straw lining. *(Gresley Society)*

The tender of Jubilee No. 45672 *Anson* has its coal re-stacked. Safety valves are feathering indicating a good head of steam. The livery is the first adopted by British Railways of black with maroon and straw lining. Unusually for Camden the engine carries an excursion headboard for *Motor Cycling Magazine's* excursion to the Isle of Man for the TT races. *(G. Powell/Gresley Society)*

At the rear of the shed yard, a trio of Pacifics stand ready for their next turns in June 1963. Most prominent is No. 46256 *Sir William A. Stanier F.R.S.* The tenders of the other two are of ex-streamlined engines, as the ladders and extended side sheets show. *(D. Loveday)*

The care taken on shed with the pride of Camden, No. 46245 *City of London,* is obvious in the engine's appearance. Behind the loco is Camden's water tank, 1959. *(R. K. Blencowe)*

Camden's No. 46242 *City of Glasgow* displays the headboard of the Euston–Heysham train for Belfast sailings. After repair following severe damage in the Harrow rail disaster, a new curved section over the buffer beam replaced the cut-away version. *City of Glasgow* then carried its third version of front end. 15 June 1957. *(R. K. Blencowe)*

Ready for the road, No. 46209 *Princess Beatrice* faces north at the top end of the shed. For an engine in such good condition to go for scrap, in the following September, shows the short-sightedness of management decisions. April 1962. *(D. Loveday)*

The cycle begins once more; No. 46234 *Duchess of Abercorn* leads a cavalcade down to Euston. The middle loco is No. 46206 *Princess Marie Louise*, identified by its tender coal pusher (the only one of the class to have one fitted). Working as a trio to save line occupancy, they separated at Euston. Photographed July 1962. *(D. Loveday)*

A final glimpse of Camden with four Duchesses and a Britannia on shed. Only No. 46246 *City of Manchester* can be identified; its chimney is covered which is an ominous sign. April 1963. *(D. Loveday)*

Departures from London Euston

To gain access to the departures side of the station, travel or platforms tickets needed to be presented before entry was allowed through the iron lattice gates of Platform 12. For those wishing to take photographs it proved disappointing as the distance obtainable did not get a good picture.

At buffer stops the engine from 1A Willesden that brought in the empty stock remained coupled up. In practice, any of the 1A engine allocation brought in the train. The engine remained coupled up in order to provided steam heating prior to the train engine itself being coupling up. The engine backed down from 1B Camden Shed and coupled up, then tested the vacuum required for the brakes. Once the train engine had coupled up, the 1A engine uncoupled and waited ready to assist in banking the train away.

As departure time approached the level of platform activity increased with catering supplies loaded for the restaurant and buffet coaches. For passengers, a visit to the Menzies bookstall to search for reading material required for the journey would be normal. Younger travellers sought out a comic book or an *I-Spy* or railway book, maybe a new *abc* spotter's book. The guard walked down the platform to the front of the train to inform the driver of the load, also to confirm departure and arrivals for stations on-route.

If the train was double-headed, the two drivers agreed the order that each engine picked up water from the troughs. Only one engine could scoop the troughs as the water levels were never sufficient for two to replenish at the same time.

After the leisurely boarding of passengers assisted by porters, they then kept a watchful eye for last minute passengers for the train. Some left the coach to walk up to the front of the train in order to see which locomotive was attached. For any younger passengers it did not take much persuasion for their fathers to take them for a closer look. In a short-lived experiment, a small paxolin notice with the driver's name was displayed on the cab side of the loco. Following comments of irate passengers on some occasions it was discontinued, although the mounting brackets could still be seen on many engines afterwards.

Shortly after the slamming of doors, a sharp shrill whistle from the guard indicated that all doors were closed in readiness for departure. Relatives and friends stood close to the coach to say their goodbyes, some holding a handkerchief that might be used to wave or perhaps to wipe away a tear. The driver acknowledged the whistle with one from the engine, the driver or fireman gazing towards the end of the train for a wave of the guard's flag to signal all doors were closed, and 'Right Away'.

As the engine stood for some time, its driver opened the drain cocks on the cylinders to empty any water which collected there as steam evaporated. Those stood around witnessed the noisy drama of departure as a cloud of steam shrouded the front of the engine. The driver gently opened the regulator and a little wheel slip generally happened as the loco's driving wheels gained adhesion. Steam power was both audible and visible as slowly the train got under way.

Banking assistance came from the 1A engine that brought in the empty carriages and heated the train prior to the express engine coupling up. The engine was not coupled up to the train, but buffered up to the rear coach to push the train.

The start of a journey from Euston proved difficult. Gradients in the first mile of the journey of 1:70 and 1:112 the first to be climbed, not an easy task for a locomotive just off shed with its fire not yet fully burned through. After a mile of banking the train passed over the gradients known as Camden Bank and the banking engine dropped off the train. This engine either returned to 1A Willesden Shed or for further duties at Euston.

Although prepared on-shed, the driver of No. 46206, *Princess Marie Louise*, oils around once more. The tender is generously filled with coal for the journey north. The fireman is in luck, as No. 46206 is fitted with a steam coal-pusher. The Mid-Day Scot was always known as 'The Corridor' to railwaymen, simply because of being the first one to have corridor coaches. *(Travel Lens Photographic)*

The most prestigious of Euston express passenger departures, The Royal Scot, headed on 24 July 1959 by No. 46221 *Queen Elizabeth*. The engine had been transferred from 5A Crewe North in June 1959. Not superstitious, the authorities always had the train depart from Platform 13. *(R. K. Blencowe)*

The driver of No. 46239, *City of Chester,* has quite a group of people around asking questions about the loco. The smokebox shed plate has gone, possibly for a souvenir as the date is April 1963. The engine was re-allocated to 1A Willesden Shed on the closure of Camden. *(D. Loveday)*

One of 1B Camden drivers' favourite engines, No. 46244 *King George VI*, pictured minutes before departure at 10.00 a.m.

The headboard is the most ornate version, with a tartan background and red lion on the shield. Other identification for the train is on the end corridor blanking board, which bore the name The Royal Scot, 4 October 1953. Still in-situ are the original wooden planks that made up the platform's surface. Just a short distance across London the Eastern Region's premier express, The Flying Scotsman also had the same 10.00 a.m. departure time. *(R. Butterfield/Initial Photographics)*

The powder-blue experimental *Deltic* made a good impression with its sheer power. The engine did a series of test runs on Liverpool trains for quite a time. Spotters could be puzzled looking for the name in their *abc* books, as it was owned by the English Electric Company. It was never in BR stock. *(Gresley Society)*

Surrounded by steelwork, No. 46249, *City of Sheffield,* blows from her safety valves indicating the engine has a good head of steam, *c.* 1949. *(Gresley Society)*

Visible evidence of the building construction changes as No. 46256, *Sir William A. Stanier F.R.S.*, gets under way. A carriage end blanking lies on what is probably Platform 11. *(Travel Lens Photographic)*

Black Five No. 44866 double-heads Jubilee No. 45647 *Sturdee*. As the Jubilee was a 3B Bushbury engine, the train is a heavily loaded Midlander express. *(Gresley Society)*

Surrounded by building works and scrap barrels, No. 46239 *City of Chester* still looks in good condition in June 1963. *(D. Loveday)*

Proof, if needed, that despite our memories suggesting otherwise it did pour with rain, as the soaking platform shows. Royal Scot No. 46150 *The Life Guardsman* moves out, in April 1963. *(D. Loveday)*

Jubilee No. 45721 *Impregnable,* fitted with a Fowler tender, heads a Bletchley train. Moving empty-stock from Platform 1 is a Fowler 2-6-2 tank engine. *(R. S. Collection)*

Banking an express departure, Carlisle-based Patriot No. 45513 is an un-named member of the class. Just visible is No. 46245, *City of London,* coupled up to its train to head north. *(R. S. Collection)*

Patriot No. 45510; whether the engine is just moving stock or on a stopping train is unclear. Distinct additions that enlarged the station are noticeable in the differing roof structures. *(R. S. Collection)*

Liverpool 8A Edge Hill-based Royal Scot No. 46110, *Grenadier Guardsman,* simmers from her safety valves in readiness for the 'Right Away', in April 1963. *(D. Loveday)*

Rugby 2A-based Black Five No. 44831 pilots an un-identified Stanier engine which is blowing from her safety valves, April 1962. *(D. Loveday)*

Two titled train departures to Liverpool, with two different versions of the Patriot class. The Empress Voyager only ran when required to suit sailings of the Canadian Pacific Liners from Liverpool (all ships of the line were named Empress of '...'). Class leader No. 45500 *Patriot* is in original form on the Empress Voyager, while a rebuilt No. 45525, *Colwyn Bay,* heads the 12.30 p.m. departure named The Red Rose, 1958. *(R. K. Blencowe)*

The footplate crew of Black Five No. 45387 of 1A Willesden Shed await instructions from the guard about stops and the train's loading. The train engine is an early diesel, 1960. *(Gresley Society)*

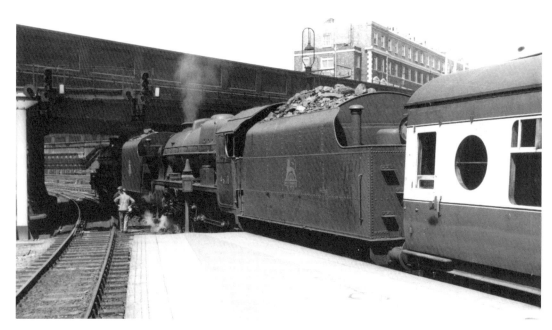

Drivers of Royal Scot No. 46138, *London Irish Rifleman,* and the un-identified Black Five are in discussion, probably about the order for pick-up from the water troughs en-route. *(Gresley Society)*

Willesden 1A Shed's Jubilee No. 45601, *British Guiana,* is piloted by a Compound 4-4-0. The Fowler tender shows the fire irons to be overhanging out of the coal space in this *c.* 1958 photograph. *(R. K. Blencowe)*

The driver of No. 46228, *Duchess of Rutland,* peers down the train to see the guard's 'Right Away' signal. Drivers at the top of the profession took pride in their appearance as this driver shows with his shirt and tie. The train is the 10.25 a.m. for Carlisle and Windermere. *(B. W. L. Brooksbank/Initial Photographic)*

The moment departure begins. The driver of Royal Scot No. 46128, *The Lovat Scouts,* opens its regulator in unison with that of pilot engine Black Five No. 44931. April 1962. *(D. Loveday)*

At the rear of the train, Black Five No. 44904, having brought in the empty stock, now assists the train engine by pushing the train up Camden Bank. At the crest of the climb the engine will fall back, either returning to 1A Willesden Shed, or Euston to do some shunting, photographed in April 1962. *(D. Loveday)*

The Locoshed book

Details of the shed locations of locomotives could be obtained from this Ian Allan book which was published twice each year. The only photograph in the whole publication is on the cover; the inner leaf has a line drawing of a Fowler/Hughes Crab.

Named locomotives are indicated by just *

This bruised example from 1959 records allocations up to November; a note inside the cover recommends to consult the magazine *Trains Illustrated* for changes. In reality, the book of ninety-seven pages was never current as many reallocations took place. It is unlikely that the book sold in vast quantities, unlike the regional engine series as 2s6d in those days proved a luxury purchase.

For those who never owned a copy they did not miss much, as it could possibly be the blandest book in the whole range of publications.

The cover photograph is of two Royal Scot engines; the main subject is No. 46148 *The Manchester Regiment.* The location is 1B Camden Shed.

(Allocations of engine sheds that had workings to and from London Euston in 1959 are detailed in the next section. All of the listings are shown: Duchess, Princess Royal Scot, Patriot, Jubilee, Britannia and Black Fives. Exceptions for work into Euston are the smaller engines, although Willesden locos or a 2P from 5A Crewe North which on occasions found its way south).

(Ian Allan Publishing)

Shed Allocations

1B CAMDEN

Summer 1959 allocation – 41 locomotives

Patriot 4-6-0:
45514 *Holyhead*
45522 *Prestatyn*
45523 *Bangor*
45532 *Illustrious.*

Jubilee 4-6-0:
45592 *Indore*
45601 *British Guiana*
45606 *Falkland Islands*
45669 *Fisher*
45676 *Codrington*
45686 *St Vincent*
45722 *Defence*
45735 *Comet*

Royal Scot 4-6-0:
46100 *Royal Scot*
46139 *The Welch Regiment*
46144 *Honourable Artillery Company*
46146 *The Rifle Brigade*
46154 *The Hussar*
46161 *King's Own*
46162 *Queen's Westminster Rifleman*
46168 *The Girl Guide*
46170 *British Legion*

Coronation 4-6-2:
46229 *Duchess of Hamilton*
46239 *City of Chester*
46240 *City of Coventry*
46242 *City of Glasgow*
46245 *City of London*
46247 *City of Liverpool*
46254 *City of Stoke-on-Trent*
46256 *Sir William A. Stanier F.R.S.*

Class 3F 0-6-0T:
47302, 47304, 47307, 47310, 47348,
47495, 47514, 47522, 47529, 47668,
47669, 47671

3B BUSHBURY

Summer 1959 allocation – 38 locomotives

Class 2, 2-6-2 T:
41225, 41279, 44439

Class 4, 2-6-4 T:
42428

Class 4F, 0-6-0:
44027

Class 5, 4-6-0:
44829, 45015, 45287, 45310, 45395,
45440S, 45439

Jubilee 4-6-0:
45555 *Quebec*
45647 *Sturdee*
45688 *Polyphemus*

45709 *Implacable*
45734 *Meteor*
45737 *Atlas*
45738 *Samson*
45741 *Leinster*
45742 *Connaught*

Class 3F, 0-6-0 T:
47363, 47397, 47398, 47473

Class 7F, 0-8-0:
48950, 49037, 49044, 49240, 49411,
49452

Class 2F, 0-6-0:
58118, 58119, 58124, 58183, 58204,
58281, 58295

5A CREWE NORTH

Summer 1959 allocation – 125 locomotives

Class 2P, 4-4-0:
40652, 40653, 40655, 40659, 40660, 40679

Class 2, 2-6-2 T:
41212, 41220, 41229

Class 4, 2-6-4 T:
42575, 42578, 42677

Class 6P5F, 2-6-0:
42946, 42954, 42955, 42958, 42961, 42963, 42966, 42968

Class 5, 4-6-0:
44678, 44679, 44680, 44682, 44684, 44685, 44714, 44758, 44759, 44760, 44761, 44762, 44763, 44764, 44765, 44766, 45000, 45021, 45033, 45073, 45093, 45113, 45148, 45189, 45235, 45240, 45243, 45250, 45254, 45257, 45282, 45289, 45305, 45311, 45348, 45369, 45373, 45379, 45390, 45434, 45446

Patriot 4-6-0:
45501 *St Dunstan's*
45503 *The Royal Leicestershire Regiment*
45528
45529 *Stephenson*
45545 *Planet*
45546 *Fleetwood*
45548 *Lytham St Annes*

Jubilee 4-6-0:
45553 *Canada*
45556 *Nova Scotia*
45591 *Udaipur*
45604 *Ceylon*
45623 *Palestine*
45625 *Sarawak*
45629 *Straits Settlements*
45630 *Swaziland*
45634 *Trinidad*
45643 *Rodney*
45655 *Keith*
45666 *Cornwallis*
45674 *Duncan*
45684 *Jutland*
45689 *Ajax*
45703 *Thunderer*
45721 *Impregnable*
45726 *Vindictive*
45736 *Phoenix*

Royal Scot 4-6-0:
46101 *Royal Scots Grey*
46110 *Grenadier Guardsman*
46118 *Royal Welch Fusilier*
46120 *Royal Inniskilling Fusiliers*
46125 *3rd Caribinier*
46128 *Lovat Scouts*
46129 *The Scottish Horse*
46134 *The Cheshire Regiment*
46135 *The East Lancashire Regiment*
46138 *The London Irish Regiment*
46150 *The Life Guardsman*
46151 *The Royal Horse Guardsman*

46152 *The King's Dragoon Guardsman*
46157 *The Royal Artilleryman*
46159 *The Royal Air Force*
46163 *Civil Service Rifleman*

Princess 4-6-2:
46205 *Princess Victoria*
46206 *Princess Marie Louise*
46212 *Duchess of Kent*

Coronation 4-6-2:
46220 *Coronation*
46221 *Queen Elizabeth*
46225 *Duchess of Gloucester*
46228 *Duchess of Rutland*
46233 *Duchess of Sutherland*
46234 *Duchess of Abercorn*
46235 *City of Birmingham*
46241 *City of Edinburgh*
46243 *City of Lancaster*
46246 *City of Manchester*
46248 *City of Leeds*
46249 *City of Sheffield*
46251 *City of Nottingham*
46252 *City of Leicester*
46253 *City of St Albans*

Class 8P, 4-6-2:
71000 *Duke of Gloucester*

Class 2, 2-6-0:
78030

8A EDGE HILL

Summer 1959 allocation – 124 locomotives

Class 4, 2-6-4 T:
42121, 42155, 42441, 42459, 42564,
42570, 42583, 42602

Class 5, 4-6-0:
44768, 44769, 44772, 44773, 44906,
44907, 45005, 45032, 45039, 45069,
45181, 45242, 45249, 45256, 45276,
45343, 45376, 45380, 45398, 45399,
45401, 45410, 45413, 45421

Patriot 4-6-0:
44415 *Caernarvon*
45516 *The Beds & Herts Regiment*
45518 *Bradshaw*
45521 *Rhyl*
45525 *Colwyn Bay*
45527 *Southport*
45531 *Sir Frederick Harrison*
45534 *E. Tootal Bradhurst*
45535 *Sir Herbert Walker K.C.B.*
45539 *E. C. Trench*
45544
45549
45550

Jubilee 4-6-0:

45552 *Silver Jubilee*
45554 *Ontario*
45560 *Prince Edward Island*
45567 *South Australia*
45567 *Assam*
45586 *Mysore*
45596 *Bahamas*
45670 *Howard of Effingham*
45678 *De Robeck*
45681 *Aboukir*
45733 *Novelty*

Royal Scot 4-6-0:

46114 *Coldstream Guardsman*
46119 *Lancashire Fusilier*
46123 *Royal Irish Fusilier*
46124 *London Scottish*
46132 *The King's Regiment Liverpool*
46142 *The York and Lancaster Regiment*
46147 *The Northamptonshire Regiment*
46155 *The Lancer*
46156 *The South Wales Borderer*
46164 *The Artists' Rifleman*

Princess Royal Class 4-6-2:

46200 *The Princes Royal*
46203 *Princess Margaret Rose*
46204 *Princess Louise*
46207 *Princess Arthur of Connaught*
46208 *Princess Helena Victoria*
46209 *Princess Beatrice*
46211 *Queen Maud*

Class 3F, 0-6-0T:

47353, 47357, 47402, 47404, 47407,
47411, 47416, 47487, 47488, 47489,
47498, 47519, 47566, 47597, 47656

Class 8F, 2-8-0:

48152, 48249, 48280, 48318, 48433,
48457, 48479, 48504, 48509, 48512,
48513

Class 7F, 0-8-0:

49082, 49116, 49132, 49137, 49173,
49200, 49224, 49355, 49366, 49375,
49392, 49394, 49399, 49404, 49405,
49412, 49416, 49419, 49427, 49429,
49434, 49435, 49437, 49445

Class 2F, 0-6-0 ST

51445

9A LONGSIGHT

Summer 1959 allocation – 105 locomotives

Class 3, 2-6-2 T:
40076, 40077, 40078, 40084, 40107, 40122

Class 2P, 4-4-0:
40674, 40693, 40093

Class 2P, 4-4-0:
41907, 41908, 42416

Class 2, 2-6-2 T:
42369, 42381, 42398, 42399

Class 4, 2-6-4T:
42369, 42381, 42398, 42399, 42416

Class 6P5F, 2-6-0:
42772, 42846, 42814, 42848, 42858, 42887, 42889, 42923, 42924, 42925, 42930, 42934, 42936, 42938

Class 4F, 0-6-0:
44061, 44349

Class 5, 4-6-0:
44686, 44687, 44741, 44742, 44746, 44748, 44749, 44750, 44751 44752, 44827, 44937, 45109, 45111, 45302, 45426

Patriot 4-6-0:
45505 *The Royal Ordnance Corps*
45520 *Llandudno*
45530 *Sir Frank Ree*
45536 *Private W. Wood V.C.*
45540 *Sir Robert Turnbull*
45543 *Home Guard*

Jubilee 4-6-0:
45578 *United Provinces*
45587 *Baroda*
45595 *Southern Rhodesia*
45631 *Tanganyika*
45638 *Zanzibar*
45644 *Howe*
45671 *Prince Rupert*
45680 *Camperdown*

Royal Scot 4-6-0:
46106 *Gordon Highlander*
46108 *Seaforth Highlander*
46111 *Royal Fusilier*
46115 *Scots Guardsman*
46122 *Royal Ulster Rifleman*
46131 *Royal Warwickshire Regiment*
46137 *The Prince of Wales's Volunteers*
(South Lancashire)
46140 *Kings Royal Rifle Corps*
46143 *The South Staffordshire Regiment*
46153 *Royal Dragoon*
46158 *The Loyal Regiment*
46160 *Queen Victoria's Rifleman*
46166 *London Rifle Brigade*
46169 *The Boy Scout*

Class 3F, 0-6-0 T:
47267, 47291, 47341, 47343, 47345,
47347, 47356, 47369, 47395, 47400,
47528, 47673

Class 8F, 2-8-0:
48165, 48275, 48389, 48428, 48465,
48500, 48680, 48744

Class 7, 0-8-0:
49428, 49439

Britannia 4-6-2:
70031 *Byron*
70032 *Tennyson*
70033 *Charles Dickens*
70043 *Lord Kitchener*

CARLISLE UPPERBY 12 B (1958–1966)

Summer 1959 allocation – 103 locomotives

Class 2P, 4-4-0:
40628, 40629, 40656

Class 4, 2-6-4 T:
42426, 42449, 42539, 42664

Class 4F, 0-6-0:
43896, 44016, 44060, 44081, 44121, 44126, 44326, 44346, 44596

Class 5, 4-6-0:
44740, 44936, 44939, 45025, 45070, 45106, 45112, 45140, 45185, 45197, 45244, 45246, 45248, 45258, 45259, 45286, 45293, 45295, 45296, 45297, 45315, 45316, 45317, 45323, 45329, 45344, 45351, 45368, 45371, 45394, 45397, 45402, 45412, 45414, 45431, 45437, 45438, 45445, 45451, 45494

Patriot 4-6-0:
45502 *Royal Naval Division*
45507 *Royal Tank Corps*
45508
45512 *Bunsen*
45513
45524 *Blackpool*
45526 *Morecambe & Heysham*
45533 *Lord Rathmore*
45537 *Private E. Sykes V.C.*
45541 *Duke of Sutherland*
45551

Jubilee 4-6-0:
45588 *Kashmir*
45593 *Kolhapur*
45599 *Bechuanaland*
45617 *Mauritius*
45672 *Anson*, 45723 *Fearless*

Royal Scot 4-6-0:
46126 *Royal Army Service Corps*
46136 *Border Regiment*
46141 *The North Staffordshire Regiment*
46165 *The Ranger (12th London Regiment)*
46167 *The Hertfordshire Regiment*

Coronation 4-6-2:
46226 *Duchess of Norfolk*
46236 *City of Bradford*
46237 *City of Bristol*
46238 *City of Carlisle*
46244 *King George VI*
46250 *City of Lichfield*
46255 *City of Hereford*
46257 *City of Salford*

Class 2, 2-6-0:
46449, 46457

Class 3F, 0-6-0 T:
47288, 47292, 47295, 47326, 47337, 47340, 47337, 47408, 47415, 47492, 47602, 47614, 47666

Class 2F, 0-6-0:
58215

HOLYHEAD 6J (1952–1966)

Summer 1959 allocation – 19 locomotives

Class 5, 4-6-0:
44661, 44802, 44986, 45056, 45110, 45382, 45429, 45441

Royal Scot 4-6-0:
46127 *Old Contemptibles*
46149 *The Middlesex Regiment*

Britannia 4-6-2:
70045 *Lord Rowallan*
70046 *Anzac*
70047 **
70048 *The Territorial Army 1908–1958* *
70049 *Solway Firth* **
(**unnamed in summer 1959)

(*In a departure from the normal brass nameplates, those of No. 70048 were made from aluminium and double-lined with a red background. The naming took place at Euston on 23 July by the Duke of Norfolk.)

24E BLACKPOOL CENTRAL (1952–1963)

Summer 1959 allocation – 39 locomotives

Class 3, 2-6-2 T:
40072, 40099, 40103, 40109, 40164, 40166, 40174

Class 4, 2-6-4 T:
42148, 42461, 42625, 42638

Class 5, 4-6-0:
44730, 44731, 44732, 44733, 44737, 44778, 44779, 44926, 44927, 44930, 44947, 44950, 44982, 44988, 45077, 45200, 45201, 45318, 45436, 45464

Jubilee 4-6-0:
45571 *South Africa*
45574 *India*
45580 *Burma*
45584 *North West Frontier*
45653 *Barham*
45705 *Seahorse*

Class 4, 2-6-4 T:
80046, 80093

The Wind of Change

Diesel traction on the London Midland Region had been tested, in the form of the LMS twins 10000 and 10001, the prototype *Deltic*, and the Southern Railway 1 Co-Co1 locomotives 10201 and 10202 in 1957. By late 1959 the ominous signs of the end of steam came with the gradual introduction of type 4 diesels.

Building commenced in 1958 on the English Electric type 4, a 1 Co-Co 1, later known as Class 40s by the Vulcan Foundry for most of the order (D200–D304 and D325–D399). *Robert Stephenson* and *Hawthorn* completed the series (D305–D324) between 1960–1961. The faith which British Railways had in replacing the steam locomotive seemed to be misplaced, as on numerous occasions it fell to steam locos to rescue ailing diesel-hauled trains.

Of the 200 engines built, just twenty-five received the names of ships of various companies. The majority carried those of Cunard liners, and all had association with shipping lines that sailed, or still sailed from Liverpool.

Named examples were allocated to the West Coast Main Line. Spotters soon got used to the new age as the spread of diesels took a hold in the West Coast Main Line depots. Where once a shed had Stanier's wonderful engines of the Duchess, Princess, Royal Scot or Jubilee classes, the Diesels type 4s began arriving in number. By the end of 1961 Crewe North had twenty-seven, Camden twenty-three, Edge Hill sixteen and Longsight fourteen.

One of the named engines, D212 *AUREOL,* is preserved at the Midland Railway Centre in her original Brunswick green livery. *(R. S.)*

The aluminium nameplates owed a little to those of the Southern Railway's Merchant Navy Class, having their centres painted in the house colours of each company. Unlike the large 6 foot 1 inch length of the Merchant Navy Class, the named D200s were only a diminutive 2 feet 4 inches. This seemed lost on such a large expanse of locomotive.

40 010 *EMPRESS OF BRITAIN (CP)*
40 011 *MAURETANIA (CL)*
40 012 *AUREOL (EDL)*
40 013 *ANDANIA (CL)*
40 014 *ANTONIA (CL)*
40 015 *AQUITANIA (CL)*
40 016 *CAMPANIA (CL)*
40 017 *CARINTHIA (CL)*
40 018 *CARMANIA (CL)*
40 019 *CARONIA (CL)*
40 020 *FRANCONIA (CL)*
40 021 *IVERNIA (CL)*
40 022 *LACONIA (CL)*

40 023 *LANCASTRIA (CL)*
40 024 *LUCANIA (CL)*
40 025 *LUSITANIA (CL)*
40 027 *PARTHIA (CL)*
40 028 *SAMARIA (CL)*
40 029 *SAXONIA (CL)*
40 030 *SCYTHIA (CL)*
40 031 *SYLVANIA (CL)*
40 032 *EMPRESS OF CANADA (CP)*
40 033 *EMPRESS OF ENGLAND (CP)*
40 034 *ACCRA (EDL)*
40 035 *APAPA (EDL)*

The sub-script letters denote:
CP for Canadian Pacific Steamships, CL for Cunard Line, EDL for Elder Dempster Lines.

Some of the later nameplates were made of resin painted to resemble aluminium.

The D numbers D 210 to D225 and D227 to D235 are those carried when introduced, these changed at a later date when the class became known as Class 40s.

As for the naming sequence missing D226, it has been suggested that the name *MEDIA* was allocated, but not applied.

Although many enthusiasts lost interest after the demise of steam, a new generation of enthusiasts took a liking to the diesel locos. Like steam locos, Class 40s were pursued around the country by spotters years later when withdrawals took hold. The nick-name of 'The Whistlers' seemed very apt as it describes the sound of the engines. The class 40s, like other diesel classes, gave many years of reliable working after initial reliability problems were resolved.

On withdrawal from service, seven made it through to preservation either officially or by the enthusiast fraternity. These are D200, D212, D213, D316, D318, D335 and D345

Unlike the steam locomotive where some engines are remembered for record breaking, the only Class 40 to have any history was D326, which headed the West Coast Postal Special on what become known as the 'Great Train Robbery'. As its driver was injured, and later died, no thoughts were ever made of preserving this engine.

The resin variety of nameplate was, no doubt, cheaper to make. Durability suffered when much of the paintwork became damaged as a loco passed through the washing plants on shed. *(R. S.)*

A New Age of Motive Power

The beginning of the electric era on the London Midland Region in 1959 saw new motive power on the Crewe to Manchester section in September 1960 initially, then Liverpool services in June 1962. On these first sections sights of locomotives painted in the electric blue livery with white roofs, raised numerals and BR logos replaced much admired Stanier steam locomotives. To enthusiasts these newcomers became a fascination, but unlike their steam predecessors, they carried no names. Some steam locomotives (those measuring more than 13 feet 1 inch in height between rail and chimney top) were banished from the line; a yellow diagonal stripe on cab sides indicated a total ban on their working south of Crewe.

Electrification work on the 25kV AC system progressed south to complete the route into London Euston. It would not be until 1973 that the whole of the West Coast Main Line to Glasgow was completed.

The AC electric fleet increased in number over several years with differing classes built by several builders ranging from Birmingham Railway Carriage, Beyer-Peacock, English Electric, North British and BR's own Doncaster Works.

The preserved example of one of the early AC Electrics, No. E 3035, later classed as English Electric Bo-Bo type 83. To enthusiasts familiar with driving wheels, valve gear and nameplates of steam engines the un-named electrics proved no substitute. *(R.S.)*

Specifically for the newly electrified London to Glasgow line, Crewe Works built the Class 87 fleet. Much to the delight of spotters this brought to an end the days of anonymous locomotives when, a short time after introduction, it was announced that the fleet would receive names. The official naming of No. 87001 *Royal Scot* took place on 11 July 1977 at London Euston by Mrs Jill Parker, the wife of Peter Parker the incumbent BR chairman. The class then became known as the 'Electric Scots', though to spotters as the '87s'. The original choice of names was inspired as they reflected those carried in steam days by a variety of engines.

87001 *Royal Scot*
87002 *Royal Sovereign*
87003 *Patriot*
87004 *Britannia*
87005 *City of London*
87006 *City of Glasgow*
87007 *City of Manchester*
87008 *City of Liverpool*
87009 *City of Birmingham*
87010 *King Arthur*
87011 *The Black Prince*
87012 *Coeur de Lion**
87013 *John o' Gaunt*
87014 *Knight of the Thistle*
87015 *Howard of Effingham*
87016 *Sir Francis Drake*
87017 *Iron Duke*
87018 *Lord Nelson*

87019 *Sir Winston Churchill*
87020 *North Briton*
87021 *Robert the Bruce*
87022 *Cock o' the North*
87023 *Highland Chieftain*
87024 *Lord of the Isles*
87025 *Borderer*
87026 *Redgauntlet*
87027 *Wolf of Badenoch*
87028 *Lord President*
87029 *Earl Marischal*
87030 *Black Douglas*
87031 *Hal o' the Wynd*
87032 *Kenilworth*
87033 *Thane of Fife*
87034 *William Shakespeare*
87035 *Robert Burns*

(*One nameplate was stolen from 87012 in 1987; the other nameplate was then removed officially).

The three locos built in 1965/66 in the 86/1 class later received the names of famous locomotive engineers:

86101 *Sir William A. Stanier F.R.S.*
86102 *Robert A. Riddles*
86103 *André Chapelon*

No. 87001 *Royal Scot*, pictured toward the end of her service at Manchester Piccadilly Station. The livery of its new owner, Virgin Trains, gained the nickname of the raspberry ripple. Bright maybe, but in some opinions it suited perfectly. *(R. S.)*

Cast from aluminium, the 87 class nameplates varied in length dependant on the length of the name.

No. 87005 *City of London*, a name proudly carried in previous days by the pride of Camden Shed, Stanier Pacific No. 46245.

No. 87015 *Howard of Effingham*, the name once carried by Stanier Jubilee No. 45670.

The naming of the 87 fleet received praise from the public as it seemed to herald a newly found pride by BR in its loco fleet. Shortly after the Class 87 namings, others followed with the Class 86 fleet receiving names; some very appropriately from former steam locos, although others had more questionable names applied to them. The change of policy also resulted in many diesels acquiring names.

Some Class 87 names later changed and comment from enthusiasts about the choices was, 'blatant commercialism'.

87012 later received the name *The Royal Bank of Scotland* in November 1988.

Although designed for Anglo-Scottish services the 87s could be observed all over the electrified system. Unlike the Stanier Pacifics the whole of the class could be sighted in just a short time, and for loco-spotters a new policy of top and tailing trains brought double the excitement of recording a new sighting.

87101 became *Stephenson* but the nameplates moved on several occasions to different locomotives. They now survive in preservation on one side of 87001; the other side bears the name *Royal Scot*. This was due to *Stephenson* being the original name carried prior to the whole class becoming known as the 'Electric Scots'.

The introduction of the Pendolino trains lead to the end of 87 passenger workings on the West Coast Main Line. In June 2005, a sad event for loco-spotters took place with the 'Farewell to 87s' train from Euston to Manchester, double-headed by 87002 and 87010. Employed on other parts of the network, many of the locos are still fit for use. Several of the 87 class are preserved: 87001 *Royal Scot / Stephenson* (depending which side the loco is viewed from), 87002 *Royal Sovereign* and 87035 *Robert Burns*, while several others have been sold for further work overseas.

The steam days with their wide variety of engines are now a part of history, but their successors proved equally popular with enthusiasts. Underlining still continues, but now with electric and diesel numbers.

Above: No. 87012, *The Olympian*, at Euston. *(Peterdaniel)*

Below: No. 87006, another Class 87 photographed at Euston in 2009. *(Peter Skuse)*

Modern traction at Euston: *Virgin Quest*, a Class 390 Pendolino operated by Virgin Trains, 2012. *(John Christopher)*